Frontiers of Europe

Russia of the Czars

Portugal of the Navigators

Imperial Visions
The Rise and Fall of Empires

Frontiers of Europe

Russia of the Czars

Portugal of the Navigators

Joyce Milton
Russia of the Czars

Henry Wiencek
Portugal of the Navigators

Preface by James Miller
Assistant Professor of History
Stockton State College

HBJ Press
a subsidiary of Harcourt Brace Jovanovich
New York, New York

HBJ Press

Publisher, John R. Whitman
Executive Editor, Marcia Heath
Managing Editor, Janice Lemmo
Series Editors: John Radziewicz, Suzanne Stewart
Editorial Production, Hope Keller

Marketing Staff: Mark A. Mayer, Jose J. Elizalde, Laurie Farber

Authors: Joyce Milton, Henry Wiencek
Picture Researcher, Janet Adams

Consultants
    Russia of the Czars: Professor James Miller
    Portugal of the Navigators: Professor Kenneth Maxwell

Design Implementation, Designworks

Rizzoli Editore

Authors of the Italian Edition
    Introduction: Professor Ovidio Dallera
    Russia of the Czars: Professor Pacifico Montanari
    Portugal of the Navigators: Professor Angela Sala
    Maps: Gian Franco Leonardi
Idea and Realization, Harry C. Lindinger
Graphic Design, Gerry Valsecchi
General Editorial Supervisor, Ovidio Dallera

© 1980 by Rizzoli Editore
Printed in Italy.

Library of Congress Cataloging in Publication Data
Main entry under title:
Frontiers of Europe.
    (Imperial visions)
    Includes index.
    CONTENTS: Milton, J. Russia of the czars.—
Wiencek, H. Portugal of the navigators.
        1. Russia—Civilization.   2. Portugal—Civilization.
I. Milton, Joyce. Russia of the czars. 1980.
II. Wiencek, Henry. Portugal of the navigators. 1980.
III. Series.
DK32.F76   946.9   79-2527
ISBN 0-15-004033-4

Contents

Preface

The Russian and Portuguese empires arose at Europe's geographical extremities and spread out in different directions—the Portuguese to the tropical expanses of Brazil, Africa, and southern Asia, and the Russian across central Asia and Siberia to Alaska. Vast cultural gulfs separated the Portuguese, with their Latin tongue and Catholic faith, from the Slavic, Orthodox Russians. Indeed, the Portuguese and Russian paths never crossed; the two states never fought a war and never even had a serious diplomatic dispute.

An examination of the Portuguese and Russian empires is nonetheless an intriguing exercise in comparative history. In the High Middle Ages, when most of western Europe rested secure from outside attack and underwent a great cultural awakening, Portugal and Russia were devoting most of their energy to protracted struggles against formidable invaders—the Moors in Portugal and the Mongols in Russia. The building of both empires represented a continuation of medieval territorial drives. Portugal's kings and knights turned the tide by the fourteenth century, and by the fifteenth century they had carried the offensive against the Moors to North Africa. The Muscovite princes, meanwhile, having "gathered the Russian lands," threw off Mongol suzerainty in the fifteenth and sixteenth centuries and began the eastward thrust that eventually brought most of Genghis Khan's steppes under Russian rule.

"Every schoolboy" has learned that the age of discovery was launched when the Portuguese developed new navigational techniques and explored the African coast in search of new routes to Guinea's gold and Asia's spices. It is less well known that Russia's czars and princes were eager to control the lucrative land routes to Persia, India, and China. Both the Portuguese and Russian monarchies were, in fact, vast royal trading enterprises, with the ruler unambiguously the chief monopolist—a role that was generally shunned by the more fastidious kings reigning in western Europe.

As their empires grew, the Russians and the Portuguese showed themselves to be clearly assimilationist in outlook and policy. Imperial Russia manifested a strong tendency to absorb alien, even enemy, populations, demanding only a profession of Orthodoxy and loyalty to the czar. Between the fifteenth and seventeenth centuries, many prominent Tatar warrior clans (including Boris Godunov's ancestors) entered Muscovite service and the Russian nobility; in the eighteenth and nineteenth centuries the Russian state was served by loyal German nobles from the Baltic provinces. The Portuguese were perhaps even more assimilationist. Overseas, they mingled their blood freely with the native peoples they subdued or enslaved, and Brazil and other former Portuguese colonies are today among the world's truly multiracial societies. Failure to maintain segregation shocked the more race-conscious visitors to the Portuguese and Russian empires from northwestern Europe—and this underscores the contrast to the English, Dutch, and French systems.

The ruling class in both the Portuguese and Russian empires openly gloried in a parasitic existence. The Brazilian slave system, fed by blacks imported from Angola and one of the most brutally exploitative in history, survived until 1889. In Russia, serfdom steadily grew more burdensome from the sixteenth century onward until it came to be virtually indistinguishable from slavery at the time of its abolition in 1861.

In the Portuguese and Russian empires, investment and the introduction of new technology were normally left to foreigners. Dutch capitalists, for example, simultaneously established mines and munitions factories in Russia and sugar refineries in Brazil during the seventeenth century. In the nineteenth century much of the capital invested in Brazil and Russia emanated from western Europe. Embracing lands of tremendous though generally untapped economic potential, neither the Portuguese nor the Russian empires proved able to withstand modernizing pressures from industrially developing western Europe in the nineteenth and twentieth centuries.

It would be difficult to find two of history's great empires less alike culturally than those of Portugal and Russia. In their social and economic structures, however, the empires share features that should impress upon us the need to search beyond superficial dissimiliarities for underlying historical patterns.

James Miller
Assistant Professor of History
Stockton State College

Russia of the Czars

In 1453 the Ottoman Turks stormed the walls of Constantinople, and the last Byzantine emperor perished, sword in hand. The fall of Constantinople reverberated through the capitals of western Europe. Suddenly the buffer that had separated the Roman Catholic world from the Moslem East was gone, and

Western rulers began to search for ways to repair the damage. Several considered forming an alliance with Ivan III, the grand prince of Moscow and the only remaining Orthodox Christian monarch.

Not much was known about Ivan, but it was widely imagined that this Eastern prince living in the

shadow of the Mongol khanate would be pleased and honored by any gesture of recognition. Western diplomats, however, failed to appreciate the Russians' pride in their Orthodox heritage, and they certainly underestimated Ivan—a shrewd, aloof ruler whose every action was governed by a vision of the great nation Russia might become.

In 1468, Pope Paul II took the lead by arranging a marriage between Ivan and Zoë Paleologus, a niece of the last emperor of Byzantium. Zoë had grown up in Rome, and the pope had reason to believe that she would persuade Ivan to embrace Roman Catholicism and take up the cause of defending Europe against the Turks. She was dispatched to Moscow with an impressive retinue that included Greek and Italian craftsmen, armorers, and architects, as well as a cardinal of the Roman Church.

When the bridal party reached Moscow, Ivan welcomed his bride-to-be and found employment for her Greek and Italian servants at his court. It soon became obvious, however, that he had no intention of changing either his religion or his foreign policy to please the powers of western Europe. On the contrary, Ivan and Zoë demonstrated that they considered themselves the true heirs of the Byzantine emperors. The Muscovite court adopted Byzantine ceremonies and manners, and Ivan claimed for himself the Greek title of autocrat and the Roman title of caesar ("czar"). Within a generation, Russian churchmen proclaimed Moscow the "third Rome"—successor to Rome and Constantinople, which had not preserved true Christianity and therefore incurred divine punishment. Henceforth, Moscow came to view itself as the last Christian empire.

Opening page, the double-headed eagle, facing east and west—symbol of imperial Russia.

"Russia! . . . How many states can match its twentieth, its fiftieth part?" rhapsodized the nineteenth-century historian Mikhail Pogodin. These pages, views of European Russia, from the grain fields of the Ukraine (below far left) to the northern plains (near left). Above far left, a river scene. Below, the Volga, the most important of European Russia's many rivers. Above, the Caucasus Mountains, in the southwestern Soviet Union. Right, a forest in the western Urals.

The determination of Ivan III, remembered as Ivan the Great, to continue the imperial Byzantine tradition underscores the long history of contacts between Russia and Constantinople. During the early Middle Ages the first Russian state had arisen at Kiev in the Dnieper Valley, near the southern end of an important riverine trade route that linked the Baltic with Constantinople.

The founders of the Kievan state were probably Varangians, or Vikings, who in the ninth century had come to dominate trade between the Black Sea and Scandinavia. According to the earliest Russian chronicles, Varangian rule was accepted voluntarily by the Slavs of the Dnieper Valley, who had migrated into the region from central Europe not long after the beginning of the Christian era. Whether the Varangians came as guests or as conquerors, they were soon assimilated into the Slavic culture of their subjects.

One of the first recorded events in Kievan history was a raid on Byzantium in 911, which resulted in a commercial treaty giving Russian merchants the right to enter Constantinople every summer. Subsequent contacts between Kiev and Constantinople steadily became closer, if not more harmonious. In the mid-tenth century, Kiev's ruler, Olga, embraced Christianity and journeyed to the Byzantine capital, where she was received by the imperial court. Olga's subjects and immediate family remained pagan, however. In 968 the Byzantine emperor, Nicephorus Phocas, made the mistake of inviting Svyatoslav, Olga's son, to bring soldiers into the Danubian basin to assist in Constantinople's campaign against the Bulgarians. Once he had seen the rich lands along the Danube, Svyatoslav grew disenchanted with Kiev, and he returned to the Balkans a year later with a sizable army, fully intending to remain. Only quick action on the part of the Byzantines prevented Svyatoslav's force from attacking Constantinople itself and persuaded the Russians to leave the Balkans.

During the reign of Svyatoslav's son Saint Vladimir, the Russians were converted to Eastern Christianity. Vladimir had compelling reasons for choosing the faith of Constantinople, among them his desire for a military alliance with Emperor Basil II, who had recently completed the conquest of Bulgaria. Vladimir's policies opened Kiev to Byzantine influences that had a profound impact on the development of Russian culture. The Cyrillic alphabet, developed by Orthodox missionaries for the benefit of Slavic converts in the Balkans, was introduced into Russia, along with comprehensive codes of civil and ecclesiastical law based on the Roman law in force in Constantinople.

At the height of its prosperity during the eleventh century, Kiev was at least the equal of the states of western Europe in cultural development and economic wealth. Contacts with the West were numerous, and Yaroslav the Wise, the grand prince of Kiev and the celebrated lawgiver of the Kievan state, married his daughter to the king of France. But Kievan Russia was soon weakened by conflicts between the wealthy merchants and landowners and the poorer citizenry, as well as by dynastic quarrels complicated by the practice of dividing land among all of

Facing page, three views of Siberia: the taiga (above) and the rugged terrain of the regions on the Soviet Union's southern border (below, left and right).

Russian exploration and annexation of Asia began in the sixteenth century. This page, landscapes of this vast region: the Yenisei River of central Siberia (top), the subarctic evergreen forest known as the taiga (immediately above), and the picturesque country on the border of the Soviet Union and Mongolia (below).

The cathedral of St. Sophia in Kiev is Russia's oldest church. Despite extensive eighteenth-century additions, much of the original edifice, completed in 1037, remains intact. The ornate central dome (above), symbolizing Christ, is surrounded by twelve lesser domes representing the Apostles. Interior decorations (below) are the work of Greek and Russian artists.

a ruler's surviving sons. Moreover, Kiev was exposed to waves of nomadic invasions from the Eastern steppes. Especially troublesome were the Turkic-speaking Polovtsy (known in Byzantine history as the Cumans). Vladimir Monomakh, a great-grandson of Saint Vladimir, was said to have led no fewer than eighty campaigns against this persistent enemy.

Vladimir Monomakh's twelve-year reign (1113–1125) earned him a heroic reputation—one English historian has called him the King Alfred of Russia—but after his death the decline of Kiev accelerated, and the center of Russian political and economic life shifted northward, principally to the cities of Novgorod, Suzdal, and Vladimir. The dispersal of Russian power was hastened after 1220 by the appearance of a powerful nomadic people from the East, the Mongols. By 1240 the Mongols had overrun most of Russia, destroying Kiev and other major cities, ruining productive farmland, and killing thousands. Their onslaught almost completely severed the Russians from western Europe, where medieval civilization was just entering its most glorious period.

After their initial campaign of conquest, the Mongols were content to remain on the southeastern Russian steppes, where they established a khanate known as the Golden Horde. The khanate concentrated on

ПЛѢНЪРОУСКЫ

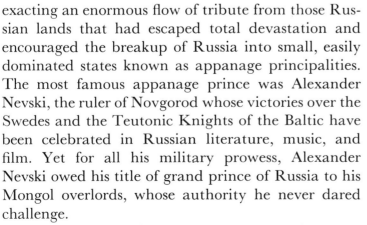

Above, a depiction of Svyatoslav, the tenth-century Kievan prince who allied himself with Byzantium to defeat the Bulgarians. Right, an episode from the life of Olga, the mother of Svyatoslav. Olga is seen ordering ambassadors from the Drevlane, an East Slavic tribe, to be buried alive in retribution for her husband's death at the hands of the Drevlane. Above right, Saints Cyril (above) and Methodius (below), the Byzantine missionaries who created the first written alphabet for the Slavs and translated much Greek theological and legal literature into Slavic.

exacting an enormous flow of tribute from those Russian lands that had escaped total devastation and encouraged the breakup of Russia into small, easily dominated states known as appanage principalities. The most famous appanage prince was Alexander Nevski, the ruler of Novgorod whose victories over the Swedes and the Teutonic Knights of the Baltic have been celebrated in Russian literature, music, and film. Yet for all his military prowess, Alexander Nevski owed his title of grand prince of Russia to his Mongol overlords, whose authority he never dared challenge.

Alexander Nevski's Novgorod was initially the most important of the appanage states. Because it was distant from the center of Mongol power and accessible to seaborne trade with northwestern Europe, Novgorod grew into a prosperous commercial city controlling much of northern Russia. Its active civic life was dominated by wealthy merchants and their families. Ultimate sovereignty was declared to reside in a general assembly of all citizens, known as the *veche,* but in practice Novgorod was ruled by a town council, which consisted primarily of leading merchants acting through an elected mayor. The hereditary prince was responsible for military defense but had to reside outside the city walls and could not

и҃ красотоу· црьковноую· и пѣньа· и слоубы· а
рхиер҃иискы· и престоианьиѥ дыиаконъ· сказоую
щеслоуженнеѥ б҃а своѥ· ѡ нже въ изоумѣнии
бывше· и оудивиша· и похвалиша слоубоу и҃:·

И призвавшаи҃ ц҃рь· василии· и коста҃нтинъ· рѣсла
имъ· идѣтаꙁемлю свою· и ѡпоустиша съ дары
велими· и чтью· ѡ нже придоша ꙁемлю· и созва
ц҃рь боꙗры своꙗ· и старци· а рѣволомеръ· се прин ша пола
ни нами моу· да слыши ѡ ни бывшее· и рѣскажи
те прѣд нами ѡ жиною·:·

Left, a page from the **Radziwill Chronicle** *showing Russian envoys marveling at the splendor of a Byzantine church (above) and reporting back to Prince Vladimir (below). This sequence is part of a legendary account of how Vladimir came to choose Orthodoxy over Judaism, Catholicism, and Islam in the tenth century.*

Above, Olga, the tenth-century princess who was canonized as the first Russian saint of the Orthodox Church. Below, Olga's grandson Saint Vladimir, who in the late tenth century made Orthodox Christianity the official religion of Russia.

acquire income or properties not approved by the council. For a time, Novgorod even established a form of the jury system, and certain court cases were decided by a panel consisting of five commoners and five aristocrats.

Eventually, Novgorod was undone by its own success. As trade increased, so did the gap between rich and poor citizens, embroiling the government in a bitter struggle between aristocrats and the great mass of the people. The veche was summoned less and less frequently, and liberty-loving Novgorod was gradually eclipsed by an upstart rival—Moscow, which lay at the strategically and commercially important watershed between the Baltic and the Dnieper Valley.

In the mid-thirteenth century, when Alexander Nevski assigned the town to his youngest son, Moscow was still relatively insignificant. Yet by 1328 one of Moscow's subsequent rulers, Prince Ivan Kalita ("John Moneybags"), was recognized by the Mongols as a grand prince of Russia. Ivan Kalita's success as a tribute collector won the Mongols' confidence and, in addition, enabled him to purchase large estates and slaves.

Ivan Kalita's "gathering of the Russian lands," both peacefully and by war, was continued by subsequent Moscow grand princes. In 1380 Dmitri Donskoi won the first important Russian victory over the Golden Horde, although Mongol power was by no means broken. In the meantime, a new antagonist was emerging in the west—Lithuania, whose pagan rulers claimed much of what had once been Kievan Russia. In 1386 the Lithuanians negotiated a dynastic union with Poland and accepted Roman Catholicism, a move that left Moscow the bulwark of Orthodox Christianity in the Russian lands. Preoccupied by their quarrels with Lithuania and various appanage princes, Moscow's rulers were for some time unable to take advantage of the Mongol decline. The final break did not come until 1480, when Ivan the Great formally renounced the Mongol yoke and concluded an alliance with the Golden Horde's rival, the Tatar khanate of the Crimea.

During his long reign (1462–1505), Ivan the Great strove assiduously to consolidate his power. He firmly believed that the emperor, as God's representative on earth, should prevail over the ecclesiastical hierarchy. Ivan and his successors suppressed the growing criticism of the wealth of the Russian church, but the clergy was forced to acknowledge the dependence of the established church on the state.

Asserting the ruler's authority over the aristocracy proved more complicated. At the time of Ivan the Great and his son Basil III, the boyar class, or old aristocracy, comprised the former princes of appan-

17

age states, the Moscow nobility, and various retainers whose families had served Russian princes since Kievan times. Such men resented the grand prince's lordly demeanor and borrowed Byzantine manners and were outraged that any attempt to leave the grand prince's service was considered treasonous. As far as the boyars were concerned, their allegiance to the Muscovite prince was a voluntary compact. Moreover, they expected to receive official appointments and favors strictly on the basis of rank, a system that made it very difficult for the ruler to reward loyal and meritorious service. To counterbalance the power of the boyars, Ivan the Great and later czars created a new service nobility, consisting of men who were awarded *pomestiya,* or nonhereditary estates, on the condition that they supply the grand prince with men for military service.

The struggle between the boyars and the grand prince reached a fever pitch during the reign of Ivan IV (1533–1584), known as Ivan the Terrible. Only three years old when his father, Basil III, died, Ivan grew up under the influence of two prominent boyar families, the Shuiskis and the Belskis. In public young Ivan was treated with deference; in private he was the butt of contemptuous remarks, even acts of cruelty.

Left, three scenes of Novgorod's miraculous victory over Suzdal in 1169. This famous icon was painted in the fifteenth century, when Novgorod was facing a still more formidable rival—Moscow. Below, two details from the Radziwiłł Chronicle *showing the Polovtsy—members of a Turkic tribal confederation—carrying off Russian prisoners and livestock (left) and the punitive raid organized by the Russians in retaliation (right).*

The austere churches of Novgorod express the spirit of this mercantile city of northern Russia. The eleventh-century cathedral of St. Sophia (near right) set the style for plain, whitewashed church exteriors. The cathedral of St. George (below far right) was built for use by the princes of Novgorod after they were forbidden to enter the cathedral inside the town walls. Above far right, the church of the Savior, near Novgorod.

Ivan's reign began auspiciously. At the age of sixteen, Ivan arranged his own coronation, assuming the title of czar, which previously had been employed only in dealings with foreign powers. He married Anastasia Romanovna, a sensible woman from a respected boyar family, surrounded himself with able advisers, and in 1550 convoked the first Russian national assembly, the Zemsky Sobor, to assist in the reform of the Russian law code. In 1557 he launched an invasion of the German-dominated Baltic province of Livonia, seeking to secure a Russian outlet to the sea.

It soon became obvious, however, that Ivan had been permanently scarred by his childhood tribulations. Every personal or public crisis—the fire that devastated Moscow in 1547, the death of Anastasia Romanovna in 1560, setbacks in the Livonian campaign—intensified the czar's paranoia and touched off a wave of persecutions. The first victims of Ivan's rage were boyars suspected of treason or of planning defections to Poland-Lithuania, which was contesting Russia's effort to seize Livonia. Later, Ivan turned on his closest advisers, the hapless few who dared remonstrate with him, and even whole towns, including rebellious Novgorod, whose population was massacred in 1570. Characteristically, Ivan prefaced and

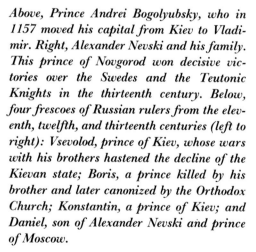

Above, Prince Andrei Bogolyubsky, who in 1157 moved his capital from Kiev to Vladimir. Right, Alexander Nevski and his family. This prince of Novgorod won decisive victories over the Swedes and the Teutonic Knights in the thirteenth century. Below, four frescoes of Russian rulers from the eleventh, twelfth, and thirteenth centuries (left to right): Vsevolod, prince of Kiev, whose wars with his brothers hastened the decline of the Kievan state; Boris, a prince killed by his brother and later canonized by the Orthodox Church; Konstantin, a prince of Kiev; and Daniel, son of Alexander Nevski and prince of Moscow.

concluded such killings by leading his servants in prayer and publicly decrying his own sins.

The combination of emotional instability and strategic brilliance that underlay Ivan's policies is most evident in a series of events that began in 1564, when the czar suddenly left Moscow and threatened to retire from the throne. In a letter that the Orthodox metropolitan was commanded to read publicly, Ivan proclaimed his love for the masses and blamed their troubles on the treachery and oppression of the boyars and clergy. Predictably, the common people of Moscow begged Ivan to return to defend them, and the boyars, realizing that they had been outmaneuvered, joined in the call. The conditions Ivan imposed upon his return ensured that the boyars would be made to suffer.

First, Ivan announced that he intended to create a unit of autonomous territories, the *oprichnina* ("lands set apart"), which would be composed of estates confiscated from the old Moscow nobility. Second, he established a new class of functionaries, the *oprichniki,* who combined the roles of a bureaucracy and a police force. Dressed in black and riding black horses with dogs' heads mounted on their saddles, the oprichniki terrorized the countryside, evicting landlords and replacing them with more tractable individuals. Often, the oprichniki set the torch to their victims' estates—and to the attached peasant villages. Towns such as Novgorod, with traditions of urban self-government, were also laid waste. In 1572, Ivan began to dismantle the entire oprichnina system, perhaps fearing that the oprichniki had become as dangerous as the aristocrats they were supposed to suppress.

Ivan the Terrible liked to present himself as a champion of the masses, and certain features of his reign, such as the summoning of the Zemsky Sobor to give the stamp of popular approval to his policies, tend to support the truth of his claim. But the pomestiye system Ivan established placed heavy burdens on the Russian peasantry. Previously, the typical peasant on a private estate had been free to move if he managed to pay his debts to his master or found another landlord willing to buy up his debt and offer easier terms for future labor. The service gentry, however, could not afford to lose potential taxpayers and military recruits, and the legal relationship between landlord and peasant evolved into one resembling that of master and serf. A series of laws was enacted tying the peasant to the land and imposing heavy penalties on anyone caught harboring a fugitive. By the middle of the seventeenth century, landlords were exerting the power of life and death over the serfs on their estates.

Of course, not every Russian commoner was a serf.

Above, the church of the Savior at Pereyaslavl, an early example of the churches built in the Vladimir-Suzdal region. The art of this district is thought to show Scythian, Georgian, and Romanesque influences. Below, a pair of richly decorated cuffs, set with pearls and enamel and woven with silver and gold threads. The cuffs were part of an Orthodox priest's vestments.

Left, Ivan I, known as Ivan Kalita ("John Moneybags") because of his success in gathering tribute for the Mongol khan (the Mongols ruled Russia from the thirteenth to fifteenth centuries). This sixteenth-century manuscript illumination shows Ivan holding court while tax collectors extract payment from his cowering subjects.

During the era of Mongol domination, Russia's monasteries grew in influence, serving as schools, centers of handicrafts, hospitals, and fortresses. Facing page, architectural monuments in Suzdal, a city northeast of Moscow (counterclockwise from top): the fortified walls of the Spaso-Evfimievski monastery; the Holy Gate of the Pokrovski monastery, erected in the sixteenth century; a fourteenth-century interior from the monastery church; and the cathedral of the Nativity of the Mother of God, inside the Suzdal kremlin (citadel).

Many peasants, especially in the northern provinces, lived on state lands and discharged their obligations to the Crown through peasant communes; these "state peasants" were usually better off than their serf counterparts. Merchants, artisans, and other town dwellers also owed direct—and typically heavy—obligations to the Crown. Under Ivan the Terrible the few urban centers that had managed to hold on to their autonomy through the appanage period were subdued.

The policies that bound peasant taxpayers to the land were developed at a time when the prospect of escape was more tempting than ever. Ivan the Terrible's conquest of the former khanates of Kazan and Astrakhan in the 1550s opened up rich new lands in the Volga River Basin and eastward toward the Urals. Despite the laws against peasant flight and the dangers of slave-hunting raids by the Crimean Tatars, the new lands were a magnet for runaway serfs. Many of the fugitives found their way to the Cossacks, free-spirited fighters living north of the Black and Caspian seas, who paid allegiance to no one but their elected ataman, or chief.

For the truly adventurous, there was the possibility of moving beyond the Urals into the vast eastern territory of Siberia. The conquest of the khanate of Sibir (located in what is now western Siberia) was a private venture undertaken in 1579 by a Cossack named Ermak Timofeev at the behest of the powerful Stroganov family, which later sponsored profitable ventures in fur trading, salt mining, and colonization. Although indigenous Siberian peoples were soon exposed to the pressures of economic exploitation and assimilation, they were never forcibly converted and, on the whole, fared better than their counterparts in the New World. The Russian colonists who began settling Siberia during the seventeenth century escaped enserfment, which was not profitable under Siberian conditions. Siberia thus developed as a frontier region in which the harsh realities of everyday life gave rise to a spirit of enterprise and individualism.

Ivan the Terrible's tumultuous reign greatly expanded Russia's domains and strengthened the power of the czar, but it left the dynasty exhausted. In 1581, a year before he was finally forced to concede defeat to Sweden and Poland-Lithuania in the Livonian War, Ivan murdered his heir apparent in a fit of anger. At his death in 1584, Ivan—who had married seven times—was survived by only two sons. The first, Fëdor, was an imbecile dominated by his advisers, especially Boris Godunov, the able and ambi-

Above, Dmitri Donskoi, the Muscovite prince who led the Russians to their first significant victory over the Mongols at Kulikovo Pole in 1380. Left, a few of the many ornate onion-shaped domes of the cathedral of St. Basil the Blessed in Moscow. This sixteenth-century church was built by Ivan the Terrible to celebrate the capture of Kazan and Astrakhan from the Mongols.

tious son of Christianized Tatar parents. Ivan's second son, Dmitri, died in 1591 at the age of nine, apparently after stabbing himself during an epileptic fit. When Fëdor died in 1598 the line of Ivan Kalita came to an end and the way to power lay open to Boris Godunov.

Under other circumstances, Boris Godunov might have made a successful czar, but Russia at the turn of the seventeenth century was still suffering from the dislocations of the reign of Ivan the Terrible. In addition, a cycle of droughts, famines, and epidemics struck soon after Godunov's accession. Many Russians were led to believe that the country was being punished for allowing a usurper to claim the throne. It was whispered that Godunov had ordered the assassination of Ivan's son Dmitri but that the child had survived and was still alive. As the rumor spread, so did an almost messianic longing for the true czar, who could redeem Russia from its troubles.

A Czar Dmitri soon appeared in the person of a red-haired ex-seminarian with a hangdog expression and a disfiguring facial wart. A more unlikely royal impostor can hardly be imagined. Surrounding himself with Cossacks, disaffected peasants, and opportunistic Polish and Lithuanian aristocrats, the False Dmitri began his march on Moscow with an army several thousand strong. When Boris Godunov died unexpectedly in 1605, all resistance to the False Dmitri collapsed, and the pretender entered Moscow in triumph.

In power slightly less than a year, the False Dmitri managed to outrage the Moscow boyars by surrounding himself with arrogant Polish noblemen. The real Prince Dmitri's mother, who had at first claimed to recognize the impostor as her son, had a change of heart and denounced the youth to the palace guards. In a lightning coup on the night of May 26, 1606, the False Dmitri was murdered and a member of the eminent Shuiski family proclaimed czar.

The elevation of Basil Shuiski pleased the boyars but did nothing to alleviate the growing tide of social rebellion in the countryside. The most formidable

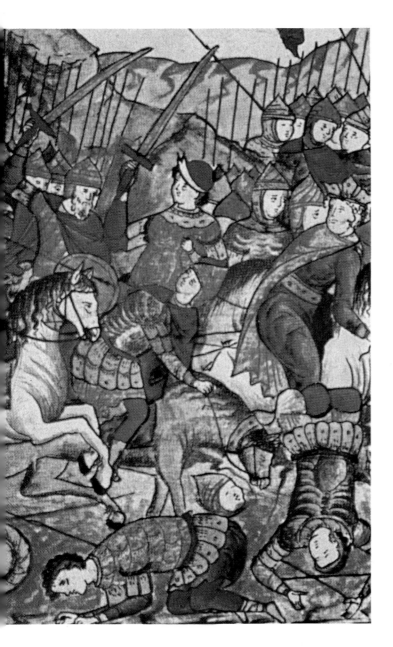

Left, Dmitri Donskoi leading his forces against the Mongols at the battle of Kulikovo Pole. Metropolitan Alexis (below) ruled Moscow before Dmitri came of age. Moscow became the seat of the Orthodox metropolitan in the 1320s, an honor that contributed to its pre-eminence among the appanage states of Russia.

rebel force, led by the slave-born Ivan Bolotnikov and Prince Grigori Shakhovskoy, soon put forward a new pretender, the False Peter, who claimed to be a son of the dead Czar Fëdor. Later, a second False Dmitri appeared and set up a court-in-exile at Tula, a city near Moscow. The opportunistic mother of Prince Dmitri recognized her lost son yet again, and the first False Dmitri's Polish wife took her place as czarina at the Tula court.

This disorderly situation inevitably presented a temptation to foreign powers. Sweden sided with the Shuiskis, while Poland-Lithuania, initially invited into the country by a faction of the Tula dissidents, soon gathered support among the other Moscow boyars. Eventually, a delegation of Moscow leaders offered the throne to Ladislas, son of King Sigismund III of Poland-Lithuania. The proposal was hedged with conditions, though, including the stipulation that the Roman Catholic Ladislas convert to Orthodoxy, and Sigismund decided that he would have Russia on his own terms.

To Sigismund's surprise, Polish-Lithuanian intervention proved to be the one threat that could rally the Russian people. Inspired by the exhortations of the clergy, the towns of the northeast raised a national army that drove the Polish force out of Moscow. In 1613 a Zemsky Sobor representing all classes was able to agree on a candidate for the throne. The choice fell to sixteen-year-old Michael Romanov, a relative of Ivan the Terrible's first wife and scion of a boyar family that had managed to keep the respect of all factions.

The accession of the first Romanov czar brought to an end the chaotic fifteen-year period known as the Time of Troubles (1598–1613). After facing near destruction, the autocratic czardom and the gentry that supported it emerged stronger than ever; the great boyars would never again be able to manipulate government policy. Poland-Lithuania, meanwhile, had lost its best chance to dominate Muscovite affairs. Before long, peasant and Cossack rebellions in the Ukraine threw Poland-Lithuania on the defensive,

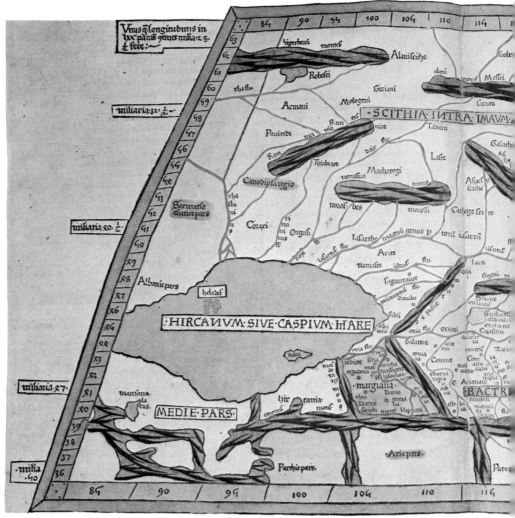

Above, the sixteenth-century church of the Dormition in Novgorod. Below, the kremlin of Pskov, an old city with governmental traditions similar to those of Novgorod. Pskov was annexed by Moscow in 1510.

The limited extent to which western Europe was familiar with Russian geography can be seen from this map (above), made in the fifteenth century. The map draws on classical sources for its description of the Caspian Sea and environs. Below, a palace in Uglich, a city on the Volga, where Ivan the Terrible's son Dmitri died under mysterious circumstances in 1591. Right, Basil III, the father of Ivan the Terrible.

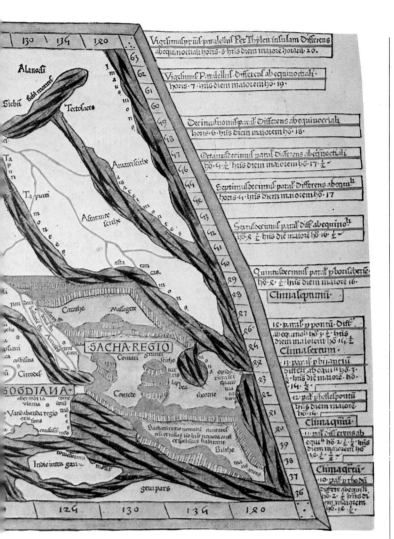

Right, Maximus the Greek, a Greek Orthodox monk of the fifteenth and sixteenth centuries who advocated a return to the spirit of the Gospel and classical learning.

and in 1654 the Orthodox Ukrainians living east of the Dnieper renounced their allegiance to the Polish king and accepted Russian rule.

The peasants received nothing in return for their patriotic service in expelling the foreigners. Indeed, the first Romanov czars rewarded the service gentry by expanding the landlord's power over his peasants. In 1649 the Zemsky Sobor was summoned, for the last time in Russian history, to approve a new law code that provided legal justification for the full enserfment of the peasantry. Some twenty years later there occurred the first of many major peasant revolts, led by the Volga Cossack Stenka Razin. Such uprisings were to be endemic in imperial Russia until 1918.

A less dramatic but equally significant development during the early years of the Romanov dynasty was the steady growth of the foreign community in Moscow. The presence of traders and artisans from abroad in Russia was nothing new, but by 1652 the number of semipermanent foreign residents in Moscow had grown so large that a special quarter of the city was set aside for them. This was called the German suburb, in keeping with the Russian practice of referring to all natives of northwestern Europe as Germans.

The "Germans" who flocked to Moscow during the seventeenth century found the Russians exotic indeed. Muscovite men with their long beards and fur-trimmed tunics struck the visitors as more Oriental than European, and the custom of keeping respectable women secluded in the *terem,* or women's quarters, reinforced this impression. Above all, the foreigners' accounts stress the contrast between the Russians' extreme piety and their uproarious public behavior.

Some Russians ate no food on weekdays during Lent, and churchgoers stood uncomplainingly through interminable services. One foreign clergyman, Paul of Aleppo, reported having attended a lit-

This page, treasures from the reign of Ivan the Terrible. The Crown of Kazan (above) was made in Moscow, perhaps by Mongol artisans captured during Ivan's conquest of Kazan in 1552. It is of gilded and painted basswood. Left, a side view of the czar's throne, with its elaborately carved wooden canopy. Below, the finely wrought gold binding of a Gospel.

urgy that lasted from eight in the morning until three in the afternoon, adding incredulously: "Who would have thought that they would thus go beyond the devout anchorites of the desert?" Manners outside of church were another matter. The Russians had always been fond of strong drink, and as early as the reign of Basil III a foreign ambassador had advised that "he who wishes to escape too long a drinking bout must pretend that he is drunk or asleep. . . ." Public and private drunkenness was a scourge throughout the country.

There is no question that the cultural gulf between Russia and western Europe was wide. The Russians had been cut off from the influence of Western feudalism and chivalry and had heard only faint echoes of the Renaissance and the Reformation. When a religious schism occurred in the mid-seventeenth century, it focused on questions most western Europeans found arcane, such as whether the sign of the cross should be made with two fingers or three. Significantly, it was the church hierarchy that favored liturgical reform and the dissenting Old Believers who clung to the status quo. Behind such seemingly trivial disputes, however, the real issue was the extent to which the state could dominate the church and dictate "innovations." Some of the Old Believers chose self-immolation rather than submit to the state church.

Russian xenophobia—the mentality of a beleaguered Orthodox stronghold—remained a major barrier to the adoption of Western ideas in education, economy, and fashion. Few Russian schools taught scientific and technical subjects. Industries such as iron founding and gunpowder manufacture were still in their infancy and largely under foreign control. Such Western fashions as tobacco smoking and tulip cultivation had caught on among the upper classes, but many Russians stood opposed to more substantial borrowings.

Among those who were convinced that Russia would inevitably have to westernize or perish was the czar known to history as Peter the Great. As an adolescent, Peter spent a great amount of his time in Moscow's German quarter, fascinated by the easygoing social life and the technical knowledge of its residents. Prodigiously energetic, he liked to work with his hands and to master the fine points of mechanical operations; in his mature years he boasted of knowing fourteen trades, including carpentry, masonry, and dentistry. In 1697, three years after emerging from a

Below, a carved panel from the czar's throne, depicting the campaigns of Vladimir Monomakh, a twelfth-century Kievan prince.

Above, Ivan the Terrible, who ruled for over fifty years in the mid-sixteenth century. Ivan's reign was a turbulent period in Russian history.

Russian icons

Orthodox Russia inherited from Byzantium the art form of the icon—a representation of a sacred personage or event, itself regarded as sacred. The greatest period of Russian icons began in the late fourteenth century, when Theophanes the Greek came to Russia, bringing his Byzantine training to the freer atmosphere of Novgorod. Theophanes' habit of painting from imagination rather than copying accepted models made a deep impression on his contemporaries. Ultimately, however, artistic experimentation conflicted with the belief that icons should reflect the immutability of truth. In the imperial workshops established by Ivan the Terrible, painters worked under close supervision.

Above, a fifteenth-century icon of Saints Frol and Lavr, protectors of horses and cattle. This Virgin and Child (right) is one of the few surviving works by the great master Andrei Rublev (ca. 1360–1430). Rublev, a monk who worked in Moscow under the tutelage of Theophanes the Greek, developed his own distinctive style, emphasizing delicacy of line, purity and harmony of color, and restrained spirituality.

Above, Saint George slaying the dragon, as depicted in a fifteenth-century icon of the Novgorod school.

Left, a detail from a sixteenth-century icon of the Last Supper. In Byzantine tradition, a representation of the Last Supper was placed on the large ("royal") doors of the screen dividing the sanctuary from the nave. Other icons on the royal doors depicted the Evangelists and the Annunciation.

Top right, Saint John the Baptist, in a fifteenth-century icon by Theophanes the Greek. Immediately above, a large icon (approximately 93 by 72 inches) depicting the archangel Michael. Along the sides of the icon are scenes representing deeds associated with the archangel.

complicated wrangle over the succession as the effective ruler of Russia, Peter left on an unprecedented journey abroad.

Peter traveled to Europe under the alias Peter Mikhailov. No one he met was permitted to acknowledge "Minheer Mikhailov's" true identity, but since the czar stood almost seven feet tall and was accompanied by a retinue of two hundred and fifty servants, his presence did not go unnoticed. The widow of the Elector of Hanover, who entertained Peter on his journey, wrote warmly of his "great vivacity of mind" but added that "it could be wished that his table manners were a little less rustic."

Peter celebrated his return from Europe in 1698 by cutting off the long and distinctly un-European beards of the Moscow boyars. He introduced modern dentistry by extracting teeth from reluctant courtiers, and he pushed through a reform of the Russian calendar—overruling the objections of the pious, who warned that he was "stealing time" from God. For the first time, ladies were commanded to appear at court social functions.

Some better-educated Muscovites welcomed the adoption of Western fashions, but Peter's innovations and his decision to abolish the Moscow patriarchate and place the church under a secular bureaucracy

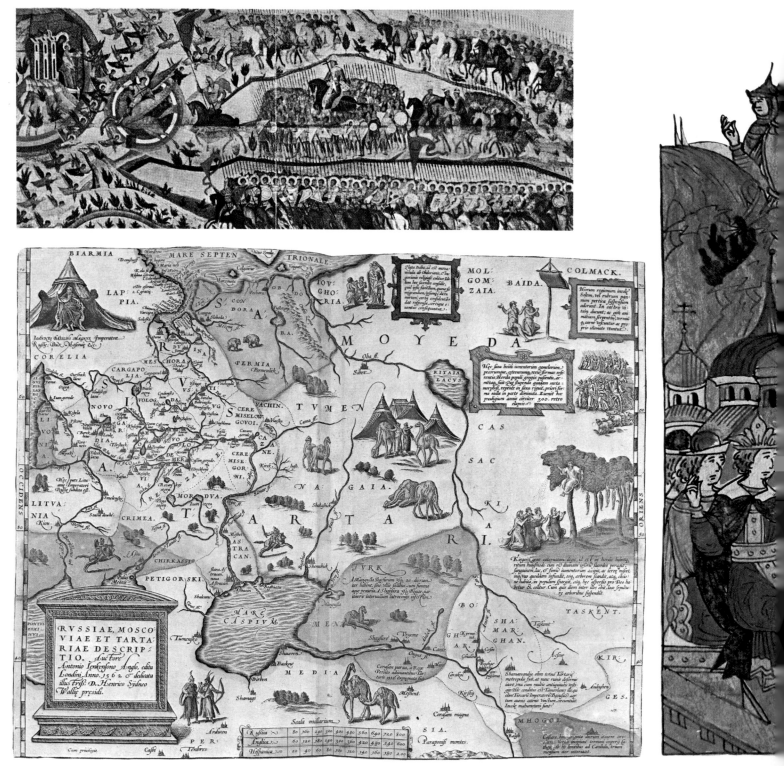

convinced many less sophisticated Russians that he was Antichrist, come to subvert Holy Russia. The controversy over Peter's policies that began in the czar's lifetime continues to this day. Russians are still divided between Peter's admirers, who praise him for having propelled his country into the modern world, and his detractors, who condemn him for having torn Russian culture from its roots and forced it into alien patterns.

Peter's ruthless suppression of a guards' rebellion in 1698 may superficially recall the ways of Ivan the Terrible, but Peter's concept of rule was quite different from Ivan's. Peter conceived of the state as an entity of laws that members of classes—and the czar himself—must serve, and he solicited the advice of the German philosopher Gottfried Wilhelm von Leibnitz in his attempt to remodel the institutions of government along Western lines. The laws requiring the gentry to serve for life as military officers were never more strictly enforced, and Peter also attempted to place government officials on salary so that the temptations of corruption would be eliminated.

By far the most important innovation of Peter's reign was the reorganization of the military. Previously, Russia's only standing army had been the regiments of *streltsy*, politically volatile part-time sol-

Above far left, angels bearing laurel wreaths to greet the conquerors of Kazan. Near left, Ivan meeting ambassadors from Kazan. Above, Ivan arriving at the monastery of the Trinity. Below, Russian soldiers of the period. Below far left, an illustrated map, dated 1562, by the English traveler Anthony Jenkinson.

Above, Fëdor Romanov, father of Michael, the first Romanov czar. Also known by his monastic name, Philaret, Fëdor was made patriarch of Moscow in 1619 and came to exercise both ecclesiastical and political rule. Right, the assassination of Dmitri, a son of Ivan the Terrible, as imagined by a seventeenth-century artist. The circumstances surrounding Dmitri's death are still unclear to historians.

Left, the capture of Novgorod by the Swedes in 1611. Sweden, at the time one of the great powers of Europe, seized Novgorod during Russia's Time of Troubles (1598–1613). After eight years of Swedish occupation, Novgorod was ransomed by Czar Michael Romanov for twenty thousand roubles.

diers who functioned as palace guards and Moscow policemen. Peter introduced the system of recruiting serfs, state peasants, and townspeople to serve for life in the Russian army—a harsh form of conscription that remained in force until the late eighteenth century, when the term of service was reduced to twenty-five years. The Russian navy, which had consisted of only one dilapidated vessel at the time of Peter's accession, grew rapidly until it numbered forty-eight warships and many more supporting craft.

The development of a navy reflected the fulfillment of a centuries-old dream—the opening of trading outlets on the Baltic, for which Ivan the Terrible had striven in vain. Seeing his chance to break the Swedish hold on the Baltic, Peter joined forces with Poland-Lithuania, Saxony, and Denmark-Norway in the protracted conflict known as the Great Northern War (1700–1721).

No one expected Russia to play a dominant role in the war. But Charles XII of Sweden made the mistake of underestimating Russian power, and in 1708 he attempted an invasion through the Ukraine, only to find himself stranded and threatened by the approach of winter. The next year a well-rested Russian force met the outnumbered Swedes at Poltava in the Ukraine and won a decisive victory.

Poltava altered Russia's position in the world. The sudden emergence of Russia as a military force of the first rank was viewed with consternation throughout Europe. One year after the battle, Peter married his niece Anna to the duke of Kurland, a principality in present-day Latvia. For centuries, members of the Russian ruling family had married within the country; from this point on, however, in keeping with Russia's new status as a European power, they would make foreign—usually German—marriages. By 1721, Peter confirmed the transformation of Russia into a Western-style empire by assuming the title of *imperator* ("emperor").

Even before Poltava, Peter had begun construction of a new capital for Russia at the mouth of the Neva River, on land wrested from the Swedes. St. Petersburg, founded in 1703, was declared by Peter to be a "paradise," but this opinion was hardly shared by the laborers conscripted by the thousands to work in the freezing marshes of the Neva delta. Nor did the city appeal to the nobility, who were commanded to establish residences there at their own expense. St. Petersburg, destined to become a rich and ostentatious capital, stood as a symbol of the heavy human cost of Peter the Great's policies. Even many Russian thinkers who admired Peter and approved of the goal of westernization were troubled by a ruler who attempted to reorder society through executive fiat.

Above, Michael Romanov on horseback. Michael was sixteen years old when he was unanimously proclaimed czar by a seven-hundred-member Zemsky Sobor in 1613. Below, the coronation ceremony of Michael Romanov. Following pages, the church of the Transfiguration, an all-wood structure on the island of Kizhi in Lake Onega (northern Russia).

Czar Alexis (far left), the son of Michael Romanov, extended Russia's borders in the east and introduced a number of reforms—many of which placed new burdens on Russia's peasantry. His son Fëdor III (near left) died childless in 1682 after a stormy six-year reign.

Left, Natalya Narishkina, the second wife of Alexis and the mother of Peter the Great.

Of all Peter's measures, no doubt the most ill considered was his decree that henceforth every Russian sovereign would choose his own successor; the edict was to result in manipulation of the succession by palace cliques throughout the eighteenth century, until the law was annulled by Paul I in 1797. Peter's decree was motivated by his deep disappointment in his eldest son, Alexis, an indolent young man who opposed his father's reforms but had neither the cunning to keep silent nor the strength to take an independent stand. In 1716, Alexis fled to the court of the Holy Roman emperor Charles VI, but two years later he was lured home and tried for treason. He died in prison after having been tortured.

Peter never in fact nominated a successor. Not until January 1725, when he was fatally ill, did he at last accept the necessity of making a will and arranging his affairs. Before slipping into his final coma, the emperor got no further than "I leave all. . . . "

Peter's advisers quickly placed his widow on the throne. The new empress, Catherine I, was a former servant girl whose inelegant manners and humble birth made her the object of ridicule. Appearing in a gown tastelessly laden with jewels and miniature icons, Catherine was described by one malicious observer as jingling when she walked "like a horse in

harness." She survived her husband by only two years and was succeeded in 1727 by Peter II, a grandson of Peter the Great.

When Peter II died of smallpox after a three-year reign, Anna of Kurland, Peter the Great's niece, became the second woman to rule imperial Russia in her own right. Anna, a widow, arrived in Russia accompanied by a coterie of German favorites and an ambitious lover, Ernst Johann Biron, whose use of the police to persecute religious dissenters and political opponents evoked universal censure. In 1741, Anna's chosen successor, Ivan VI, was deposed and replaced with Peter the Great's daughter Elizabeth, an avid Francophile. Although Elizabeth drove Russia to the brink of financial ruin with her free-spending ways, she retained popular support.

Given Elizabeth's dislike of Prussia, against which Russia fought in the Seven Years' War (1756–1763), the empress must have had some apprehensions about the young man she chose to follow her on the throne. The future Peter III, Elizabeth's nephew and Peter the Great's grandson, had been born in the German duchy of Holstein-Gottorp and viewed everything Russian with ill-disguised contempt. The young Peter worshiped Russia's archenemy, Frederick the Great of Prussia. When he became emperor

Above, the renowned Trinity-St. Sergius monastery in Zagorsk, northeast of Moscow. Below, frescoes from the monastery. Left, Avvakum, a preacher who opposed the liturgical reforms of Nikon, the patriarch of Moscow, and was burned at the stake in 1682.

Treasures of the Kremlin

Even in the darkest moments of Russia's history, the court of the czar has always abounded in riches. Valuable objects acquired as gifts or through conquest are enumerated in the wills of the earliest Muscovite princes, and by the late fifteenth century it was necessary to construct a treasury to house the czars' mounting wealth. Many more items were manufactured inside the Kremlin walls by icon painters, armorers, goldsmiths, jewelers, and seamstresses, who were recruited from all over Russia and worked side by side with artists from abroad.

The first years of the Romanov dynasty were the most productive in the history of the Kremlin workshops. Eager to put the Time of Troubles behind them, the Romanovs commissioned gold and silver tableware, religious objects, brocaded clothing, embroidered linens, ornate saddles, and countless other decorative objects. This activity came to a halt under Peter the Great, during whose reign most of the craftsmen were moved to St. Petersburg. After 1721 the Kremlin became a storehouse for antiquities.

Above left, Czar Michael Romanov's insignia. Below, a kovsh, or ceremonial drinking vessel, made in a Kremlin workshop as a gift for Michael Romanov from his sister.

Above, the Great Regalia of Michael Romanov, epitomizing the prestige of Russia and its newly elected czar.

The Kremlin Armory was founded during the fifteenth century to produce weapons for the czarist army. Over the years, it turned to the manufacture of ceremonial pieces and hunting weapons and became the repository of one of the world's finest collections of small arms. These include a number of seventeenth-century guns, such as hunting pieces with stocks of inlaid ivory and mother-of-pearl (above), as well as fine pistols and rifles (below).

Left, a quiver and a bow case, used by the czar on royal hunts. Right, eighteenth-century sword hilts studded with precious stones.

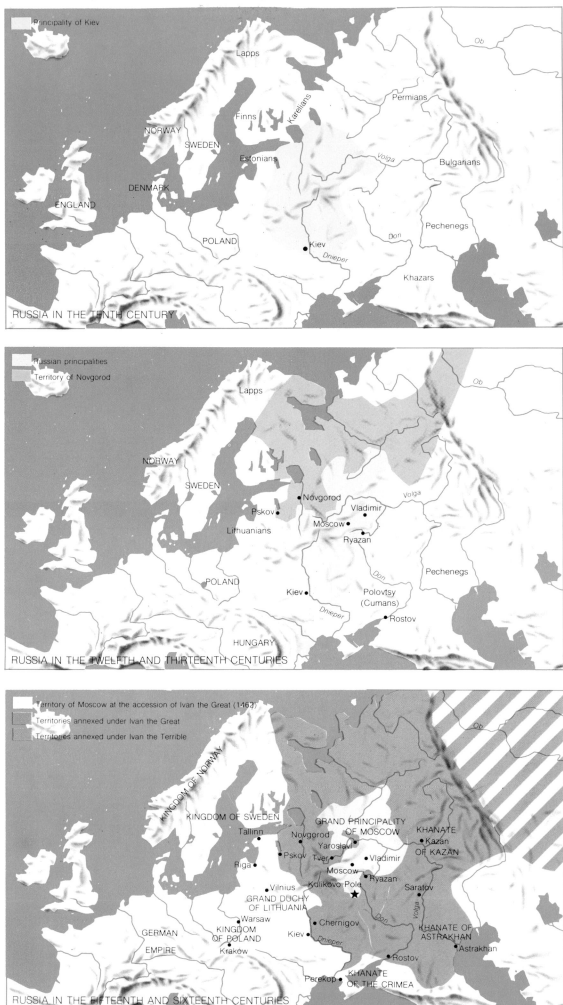

Principality of Kiev

RUSSIA IN THE TENTH CENTURY

Russian principalities

Territory of Novgorod

RUSSIA IN THE TWELFTH AND THIRTEENTH CENTURIES

Territory of Moscow at the accession of Ivan the Great (1462)

Territories annexed under Ivan the Great

Territories annexed under Ivan the Terrible

RUSSIA IN THE FIFTEENTH AND SIXTEENTH CENTURIES

Russia before Peter the Great

In the tenth century, during the reign of Prince Vladimir of Kiev (capital of the first Russian state), the Russians were converted to Eastern Christianity. Under Vladimir's son Yaroslav the Wise, Kiev's cultural influence and economic power reached its height, but strife between members of the ruling family and raids by nomadic peoples of the steppe soon took their toll. A much weakened Kiev was sacked and burned by Mongol invaders in 1240.

The next two and a half centuries are called the period of the "Tatar (that is, Mongol) yoke." Novgorod, whose prince recognized the Mongol khan as overlord, for a time flourished in the north. Its position was soon challenged, however, by the rising power of Moscow.

In 1328, Grand Prince Ivan Kalita of Moscow began the process of annexation known as the gathering of the Russian lands. During the fourteenth century the Mongol grip on Russia weakened. In 1380, Prince Dmitri Donskoi succeeded in vanquishing a Mongol army at Kulikovo Pole.

By 1462, when Ivan the Great ascended the throne, Muscovite territory was extensive and the authority of the Mongols a dead letter. Ivan added Novgorod to his domains, but further westward expansion proved impossible. In the west, however, the conquest of the khanates of Kazan and Astrakhan (1551–1556) under Ivan the Terrible marked the beginning of Russian territorial gains beyond the Urals.

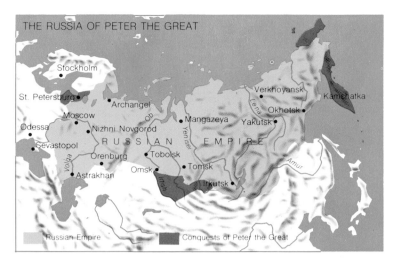

THE RUSSIA OF PETER THE GREAT

Russian Empire | Conquests of Peter the Great

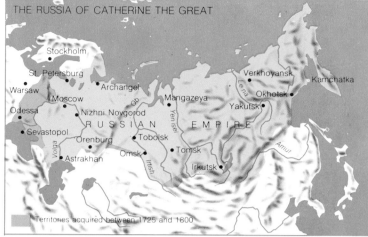

THE RUSSIA OF CATHERINE THE GREAT

Territories acquired between 1725 and 1800

Peter and his successors

In 1721, Peter the Great became the first Russian czar to be called *imperator* ("emperor")—a title entirely justified by the vast extent of his lands. Peter's Russia had a border with China stretching all the way to the Pacific and an outlet on the Baltic Sea—the "window on Europe" sought since the time of Ivan the Terrible. Domestic-

ally, Peter introduced sweeping reforms that brought Russia into the cultural orbit of western Europe.

In three partitions of Poland-Lithuania, Catherine the Great (reigned 1762–1796) brought lands that had once been part of the old Kievan state into the Russian domain. She also fought successful wars with Turkey and annexed the Crimea. Inside Russia, however, the plight of the enserfed peasantry worsened under her rule.

The Napoleonic invasion of 1812, when Alexander I was czar, threatened Russia's very survival. Overall, though, Alexander's

reign (1801–1825) was marked by continued expansion of the empire. The annexation of Georgia in 1801 provoked bitter fighting in the Caucasus Mountains.

The disastrous Crimean War (1853–1856) diminished Russian prestige abroad and contributed to demands for social change at home. In 1861, Alexander II signed an order emancipating the serfs. But the pace of the reforms soon slowed.

During the last decades of the 1800s, discontent with the reactionary government mounted. The stage was set for the transformations of the twentieth century.

RUSSIA IN THE NINETEENTH CENTURY

Territories acquired between 1815 and 1855 | Territories acquired between 1855 and 1900

upon Elizabeth's death in 1761, Peter abruptly ended the Russo-Prussian hostilities, allowing the Prussians such favorable terms that even Frederick was shocked. "I am his Dulcinea," Frederick gloated. "He has never met me, and yet he has fallen in love with me, like Don Quixote."

Peter had been emperor only a few months when his wife, Catherine, taking advantage of his unpopularity, placed herself at the head of the elite Preobrazhensky Regiment and claimed the throne. Peter surrendered meekly and was murdered soon after.

A German-born princess with no Russian blood, Catherine had made good use of the time since her arrival in Russia at the age of fourteen. She struck up numerous friendships in her adopted country, mastered the art of court intrigue, and kept abreast of the literature of the French Enlightenment. Even as em-

press she was a prolific writer who tried her hand at many genres. Astute, hard-working, and widely admired by her contemporaries, Catherine II—later known as the Great—was a woman who created her own opportunities. Once in power, she was eager to implement some of the social ideas proposed by Enlightenment writers, but she was no believer in equality and never lost sight of her own best interests.

Catherine's keen, amoral intelligence made her a superior player on the stage of international politics. Catherine completed Peter the Great's unfinished business by winning two wars against the Ottoman Turks and annexing the Crimea and a stretch of coast along the Black Sea. In the west, where Russia's once great rival, Poland-Lithuania, had declined into near anarchy, the empress pursued an even more aggressive policy. The trend of Polish history—the bolstering

Right, a mosaic portrait of Peter the Great by Mikhail Lomonosov. Lomonosov was among the outstanding scientists and men of letters of the eighteenth century. This work employs a glass mosaic technique invented by the artist. Peter the Great's first home in St. Petersburg, the city built at the mouth of the Neva River, was the Summer Palace (below left), an unpretentious two-story structure inspired by Dutch models. The much grander Winter Palace (left) was begun in 1715. Below, a coin bearing Peter's likeness.

Peter's country house

Although Peter the Great ordered the construction of several Western-style palaces, he preferred more rustic accommodations to his imposing official residences. One of Peter's favorite homes was his log cabin on Marken Island (near the White Sea port of Archangel), where he lived in 1702 while supervising the building of the Russian fleet. This *izba*, or country house, is reminiscent of the earliest known Russian dwellings and was constructed with simple hand tools.

A tradition in Russia, log buildings were by no means only for the poor. Mansions, magnificent churches, and even the sprawling Kolomenskoe Palace near Moscow were built of logs. Unfortunately, the Kolomenskoe Palace was demolished under Catherine the Great, and the nineteenth-century fashion of covering log buildings with board facings has obscured the original appearance of those wooden churches that survive.

Above, an exterior view of Peter's cabin, showing the hand-hewn slat roof. The czar's study (below) and his dining room (near right) contain furniture made with his own hands.

Above, a view from the cabin's front porch, showing the decoration of the eaves. Below, a room adjacent to the bedroom, used as a study.

Right, the sirin, a figure half woman and half bird—a popular folk motif. This example is from a painted trunk in Peter's cabin.

Left, interior views of Peter the Great's Summer Palace in St. Petersburg (counterclockwise from top): a dining room, a tiled stove in Peter's study, and Peter's bedroom. The palace is in a unique architectural style known as Petrine Baroque. Above, a pectoral ornament of the type worn by the higher Orthodox clergy. This example bears a portrait of the young Peter.

of aristocratic liberties at the expense of the centralized monarchy—was a mirror image of the rise of autocratic Russia. By the seventeenth century, the Polish legislature was crippled by a provision that allowed a single deputy, with the support of one of the great magnates, to force the dissolution of a session and the annulment of all measures passed by it. Early in her reign, Catherine had managed to have her lover Stanisław Poniatowski installed as the elective king of Poland, but when the Poles showed signs of initiating a genuine political revival, Catherine went even further. In concert with Prussia and Austria, she participated in three partitions of the Polish-Lithuanian state. The last, in 1795, removed Poland-Lithuania from the map of Europe altogether, not to re-emerge until the Napoleonic Wars of the nineteenth century. Russia gained almost all the Byelorussian and Ukrainian lands that had once belonged to the old Kievan state.

In her domestic policies, Catherine set out to strengthen the state by applying the principles of enlightened reason. The empress' written directive to the legislative committee she created in 1766, for example, was so liberal in its approach to the problems of criminology that it was banned in France. Catherine's reign saw the establishment of the first Russian

hospitals for civilians, the founding of elementary and secondary schools in many provincial capitals, and the growth of the Russian publishing industry.

But the introduction of these progressive reforms came at a time when the lot of the common people was worse than ever. Nearly half of all Russian subjects were enserfed, and serfs were bought and sold openly. Prince Grigori Potëmkin, the empress' lover and adviser, once purchased an entire serf orchestra consisting of fifty musicians. Urged to end the evils of the trade in serfs, Catherine limited herself to a decree that forbade the use of the auctioneer's hammer at public sales.

In 1773 a major peasant uprising erupted in the Ural Mountains, led by Emelyan Pugachev, a Cossack claiming to be the murdered czar Peter III. The insurgence embarrassed Catherine before her intellectual friends in western Europe and made her more attentive to the wants of the gentry landlords, who were her chief supporters. Catherine's solicitous policies were the culmination of the gentry's quiet rebellion against Peter the Great's concept of universal state service. Peter's idea that the sons of the gentry should work their way up through the ranks of the army had long been abandoned, as had the possibility of commoners entering the ranks of the hereditary

Top, a primer in Russian, Greek, and Latin, published in Moscow in 1701. Above, some of Peter's personal effects: an inlaid box containing pharmaceuticals and toiletries, and a pocket watch.

gentry through distinguished service. A law enacted during the brief reign of Peter III made gentry service in the military or bureaucracy voluntary. With that victory the landlords had become a hereditary leisure class.

Some members of the gentry used their leisure for the frivolous pursuit of French fashions; some, who delved more deeply into western European learning,

During the Great Northern War (1700–1721), Russia finally won the long-sought outlet to the Baltic. In 1700, at the battle for the Baltic fortress of Narva (below), the Swedes under Charles XII dealt a crushing blow to Russia's army. Nine years later, a totally reorganized Russian force defeated the Swedes at the Ukrainian town of Poltava (right). Peter the Great (left) displayed great heroism during the battle.

engaged in social criticism of their homeland. In 1790 the noble landowner Aleksandr Radishchev, who had been influenced by his reading of Jean Jacques Rousseau, published *A Journey from Petersburg to Moscow,* which condemned the evils of serfdom. Catherine herself annotated the book for the censor and had Radishchev sentenced to a ten-year exile in Siberia. The appearance of books like Radishchev's at home and the stirrings of the French Revolution abroad brought Catherine's enlightened despotism under fire and altered the social awareness of the Russia Catherine left to her successors.

Catherine's son, Paul I, who ascended the throne after his mother's death in 1796, soon revealed his reactionary leanings. An admirer of Prussian militarism, Paul celebrated his rise to power by turning St. Petersburg's Winter Palace into an armed camp. He began issuing a stream of edicts—forbidding travel abroad, banning the publication of foreign books, and even prohibiting the wearing of tricorn hats and other styles associated with revolutionary France. Paul's proclamations were so arbitrary and his methods of enforcement so harsh that even his closest advisers feared for their positions.

In his foreign policy, Paul was even more irrational. For a time he championed restoration of the

Above, Charles XII of Sweden. The king was a brilliant military tactician, but his early victory at Narva led him to imprudently underestimate the difficulty of defeating the Russian army.

Left, the fortress of Revel, captured by the Russians in 1710. Revel is the former name of Tallinn, the capital of Estonia. Right, a triple-barreled Swedish cannon, mounted on runners for transport over snow.

French monarchy, but he soon came under the spell of Napoleon Bonaparte. (Paul wrote Napoleon suggesting that the two "come together to put an end to all the miseries and disasters now ravaging Europe.") He developed a paranoid fear of Britain, which he hoped to attack by sending a Cossack army overland to India. In a letter of instructions to the Cossack commander, Paul openly admitted that he did not even have maps of the complete route and stated cavalierly that "it will be your business to find the required information."

This lunatic expedition helped convince influential members of the Russian administration that the time had come to find a more stable emperor. Paul's own vice chancellor led the plot, so that when the emperor asked him to investigate rumors of an impending coup he was able to say: "I have all the threads of it in my hands." Early in 1801, Paul was surprised in his private quarters and strangled, and his eldest son, Alexander, was proclaimed czar.

Strikingly handsome, the young Alexander I had been pronounced an Adonis by his doting grandmother Catherine the Great, who arranged for him to be educated by a Swiss tutor well known for his republican sympathies. Upon becoming emperor, Alexander seemed determined to translate his liberal

The multinational Russian Empire

The expansion of Russia brought into the empire a great number of national and ethnic groups, speaking more than one hundred and fifty different languages. Western Russia was the homeland of the Ukrainians and Byelorussians, whose culture had been influenced by centuries of rule by Poland-Lithuania. In the east were Mongols and Turkic-speaking tribes, most of them Sunni Moslems, as well as primitive Siberian tribesmen. The successive partitions of Poland-Lithuania during the eighteenth century made many Poles, Lithuanians, and Jews subjects of the czar. Finns, Estonians, Georgians, Armenians, and other nationalities came under Russian rule as a result of annexations during the eighteenth and nineteenth centuries. Fear that the minorities would threaten the empire with separatist rebellions prompted an aggressive policy of Russification in the last part of the nineteenth century.

An English traveler of the early nineteenth century drew these illustrations (left) of representatives of ethnic minorities in their traditional costumes. Here, they are keyed to a French map of the same period:

1. *A merchant of the Kaluga region.*
2. *An Estonian woman.*
3. *A Finnish woman in holiday dress.*
4. *A Lapp.*
5. *A Mordvin woman of the Volga Basin.*
6. *A woman from the Kazan region in Tatar costume.*
7. *A Circassian woman.*
8. *A Bukharan tribesman.*
9. *A Kalmuck.*
10. *A nomadic Kirghiz.*
11. *A tribesman of the Kurile Islands.*
12. *An Aleut.*

Above, the long façade of the Winter Palace as seen from across the Neva River. Left, the Winter Palace throne room.

The Yelagin Palace (left) was designed by the Italian architect Carlo Rossi for the mother of Alexander I in 1826. This Empire-style palace, set in an "English" park, became one of the most admired buildings of its time.

Right, the Vorontsov Palace, designed by Francesco Rastrelli, who came to Russia from Italy as a child. Built for the private use of the Vorontsov family, it later became a school for training court pages.

A window on the West

Above, an equestrian statue of Peter the Great—the "bronze horseman" of Aleksandr Pushkin's famous poem—erected during the reign of Catherine the Great.

Peter the Great's founding of St. Petersburg in 1703 marked a decisive break with tradition. Unlike Moscow, a walled medieval city, the new Russian capital on the Neva was distinguished by broad plazas, wide streets, massive stone palaces, imposing administrative buildings, and a decidedly secular atmosphere. Influenced by his admiration for all things Dutch, Peter planned a network of canals and quiet streets lined by neat private residences; even the number of windows for a given size of house was specified in Peter's master plan. After Peter's death, architects such as Francesco Rastrelli, the supreme exponent of the Russian Baroque style, gave St. Petersburg a more stately, elegant, and poetic character. Among Rastrelli's creations are the Winter Palace, the Vorontsov Palace, and the Stroganov Palace.

Above, a promenade between the Summer Garden and the Neva River. Left, Nevski Prospect and the Police Bridge over the Moika Canal. The building to the left of the bridge is the Stroganov Palace, the residence of an aristocratic family that made its fortune in the Siberian fur trade.

Top, Sophia, regent of Russia between 1682 and 1689. Immediately above, Anna, a niece of Peter the Great and empress from 1730 to 1740. Below, Empress Elizabeth, who reigned from 1741 to 1762.

Near left, Catherine I, empress from 1725 to 1727. Below left, an ornate carriage presented to Empress Elizabeth by a Cossack ataman, or chief. Right, the Agate Pavilion, designed by the Scottish architect Charles Cameron during the reign of Catherine the Great. This was just one of the splendid buildings erected at Tsarskoye Selo (present-day Pushkin), an imperial summer residence located just outside St. Petersburg.

education into effective reforms. During the early years of his reign he met frequently with a private committee of four to discuss a program of social change, including the elimination of serfdom. By 1809 he had commissioned his able minister Mikhail Speranski to submit a proposal for a constitution. Speranski responded with a well-reasoned draft, moderate in spirit but incorporating several features—such as a representative assembly with true legislative powers—that would have set Russia on the path to constitutional government.

Speranski's plan was never implemented, and in 1812 the minister was abruptly dismissed from his post, a victim of court intrigues and Alexander's waning interest in reform. Indeed, few of Alexander's ambitious plans ever came to fruition, largely because his idealistic programs, announced with great fervor, were often summarily abandoned. As he grew older, he was drawn toward spiritualism and came to see himself as the peacemaker of Europe and the incarnation of the moral power of Christian monarchy.

A born aristocrat but a dilettante soldier, Alexander was fated to become a major adversary of Napoleon Bonaparte. Alexander entered the fight determined to crush the upstart French emperor, but Russia's initial confrontation with the Napoleonic army in 1805, as part of a joint Austro-Russian force at Austerlitz (in what is now Czechoslovakia), turned into a rout that reduced the czar to tears on the battlefield. A year later the Russians were defeated again when they tried to come to the aid of Prussia. The czarist army was by no means crushed, but Alexander decided to give up a losing fight. To the surprise of the Russian people, who were swayed by state propaganda claiming that Napoleon was a false messiah, Alexander and the French emperor met on a raft in the Neman River at Tilsit (in what is now the western Soviet Union) and, in a private conversation from which all witnesses were excluded, agreed to become allies.

Below, a portrait of Catherine the Great by Dmitri Levitski. Catherine, depicted here as a lawgiver, was a noted patron of the arts.

Above, a nineteenth-century view of the square in front of St. Petersburg's Bolshoi Theater, showing a fashionable four-horse sleigh. Left, travel through a provincial village on a kibitka, a wagon on runners.

Below left, a richly decorated sled built in northern Russia during the mid-nineteenth century. Immediately below, a print depicting several types of horse-drawn sleighs.

Russian sleighs

"The cold reached seventeen degrees. The road was excellent; it was made for sleighs and we could travel very fast. Our carriages, mounted on runners, seemed to fly." Thus a French diplomat described the beginning of a journey to the Ukraine and the Crimea undertaken in the company of Catherine the Great in 1782.

Numerous types of sleighs were to be found in Russia, from rough wooden boards on runners to luxurious carriages equipped for travel over snow. Most were drawn by horses, but in northern regions reindeer or dogs were used. While foreigners may have regarded sleigh travel as a novelty, many of Russia's inhabitants were dependent on sleighs as the only practical way to transport people and goods for much of the year.

Above left, a painted sleigh from the Kostroma region of the Volga Basin. Left, a dog sled on Kamchatka, in the eastern part of Russia. Below, a two-passenger, one-horse vehicle commonly used as a cab for hire. The driver stood while his passengers rode in a sidecar.

Above, the seal of Catherine the Great. Below, St. Petersburg in Catherine's time. In 1773 the serfs of eastern Russia rose up in a rebellion that ended with the public execution of the insurgence's leader, Emelyan Pugachev, in Moscow (right). Below right, a peasant.

The Tilsit agreement of 1807 gave Russia time to pursue expansionist wars closer to home. The Caucasian kingdom of Georgia and the Romanian territory of Bessarabia were annexed, and a successful conflict with Sweden made Finland part of the Russian Empire as an autonomous grand duchy. Nevertheless, it soon became obvious that the pact between France and Russia would not last indefinitely. The Russians' halfhearted participation in Napoleon's commercial war against England (the Continental Blockade) and French interference in Polish politics were creating an explosive situation. In preparation for a Russian campaign, Napoleon built up his Grande Armée to a

strength of more than 425,000 men, many of them Polish recruits, and in June 1812 he invaded, expecting a short war and the swift capitulation of the czar. Alexander, faced with an issue unclouded by complexities, reacted with uncharacteristic firmness. "It is Napoleon or I," he declared resolutely, "we can't reign together."

But even as Alexander, in St. Petersburg, vowed that he would never surrender as long as a single French soldier remained on Russian soil, Napoleon's troops were steadily advancing toward Moscow. The Russian strategy of retreat, so often praised for its brilliance, was born of necessity. When the Russian

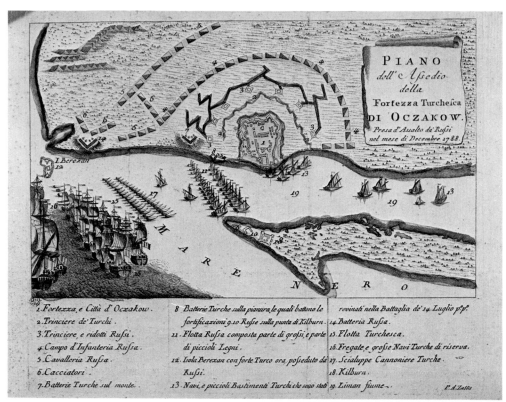

St. Petersburg was briefly threatened in the late eighteenth century by the armies of Gustavus III of Sweden (above). Below, a naval engagement between Swedish and Russian forces. Right, the Russian fleet under Grigori Potëmkin besieging the port of Ochakov on the Black Sea during a war against the Turks.

general Mikhail Kutuzov did engage Napoleon's forces at Borodino on September 7, the result was a battle that claimed nearly one hundred thousand casualties on both sides without preventing the French advance. Two weeks later, Napoleon entered Moscow—but instead of the triumphal welcome he had envisioned, he found a deserted city. The next night, Moscow's wooden houses and churches were devastated by a fire, perhaps set by the departing Russian commander. Unable to secure the treaty he had counted on and with his supply lines long since cut, Napoleon was forced to retreat through a hostile and largely barren countryside. Impeded by winter snows

and harried by partisan fighters, only about thirty thousand men survived the flight back to Poland.

The loss of his army proved to be the turning point in Napoleon's career. Austria and Prussia deserted the French cause and joined Russia and England in the alliance that in 1814 drove Napoleon from his throne. At the Congress of Vienna (1814–1815), which met to redraw the map of Europe, Alexander presented himself as the savior of Europe. He talked privately of his plans to free Russia's serfs and agreed to a surprisingly liberal constitution for the new kingdom of Poland, which was to be linked to Russia by a dynastic union. The behavior of the czar convinced

many western Europeans that he was the shining knight of liberalism.

It soon turned out, however, that the new order Alexander hoped to bring forth was the Holy Alliance, in which the rulers of Europe would agree to respect the precepts of Christian truth, keep the peace, and treat their subjects as "children." With the notable exception of England, whose foreign minister dismissed the alliance as a "piece of sublime mysticism and nonsense," the governments of Europe were willing to go on record as being in favor of Christian brotherhood. But the pact, if indeed it meant anything at all, was no more than a call for established monarchies to band together in opposition to popular movements.

At home, meanwhile, Alexander quickly disproved rumors that he intended to free the serfs as a reward for their patriotic resistance to Napoleon. Preoccupied with mysticism, Alexander began to rely on his stern and conservative adviser Aleksei Arakcheev, a holdover from the despotic reign of Emperor Paul. As for the serfs, the czar assured them that they could expect their reward from God.

Alexander's aloof behavior exacerbated the discontent of those who had suffered during the war. All classes felt cheated—from the serfs, who had lost their crops and homes, to the landlords and merchants, whose export profits had been cut off during the years when Russia was participating in the Continental Blockade. But the best-organized opposition developed among aristocratic army officers, veterans of the wars of 1812–1814, who began forming secret societies to discuss their hopes for a constitutional regime.

When Alexander died unexpectedly in December 1825, the secret societies saw a chance to use the confusion over the succession to advance their cause. Having no sons, Alexander had decided to leave his throne to his brother Nicholas, passing over Constantine, a brother older than Nicholas who had made an unsuitable Polish marriage. But before Nicholas could be confirmed as emperor, rebellious officers rallied several thousand of their troops who thronged Senate Square in St. Petersburg shouting for "Con-

Paul I (above), the son of Catherine the Great, was an unstable emperor who issued a wave of petty decrees reorganizing court life. Paul's reactionary tendencies, paranoid fears, and unrealistic plans to invade India finally convinced his son Alexander to join in the coup that dethroned and assassinated the czar in 1801. Left, Maria Fëdorovna, Paul's second wife.

By the early nineteenth century, the rivalry between Russia's two greatest cities had come to reflect the dispute between the advocates of westernization and the Slavophiles: St. Petersburg (above right) was the residence of the French-oriented court and the center of Russian cultural life, while the former capital of Moscow (right) was regarded as a repository of old Russian values.

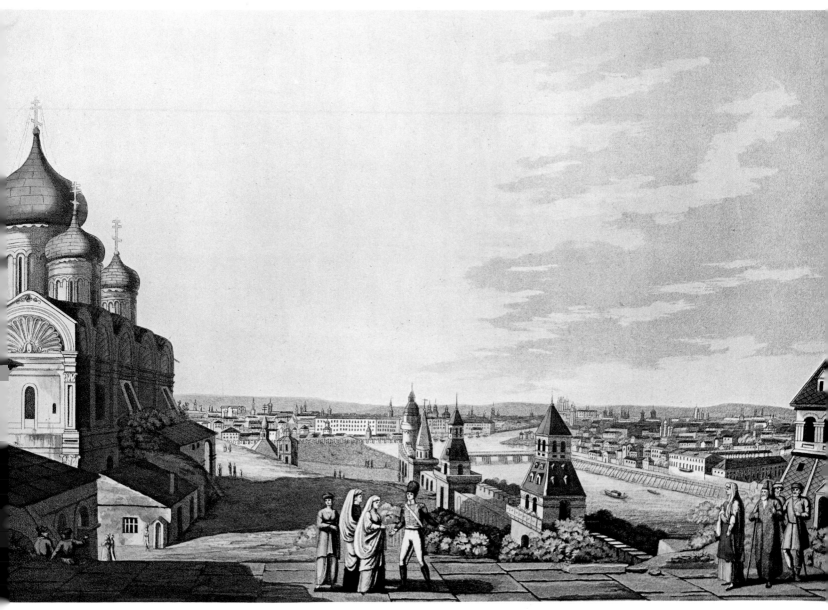

stantine and the Constitution." (The often repeated story that some of the demonstrators thought that "Constitution" was Constantine's wife may well have been an invention of conservative propagandists.) The "Decembrist" revolt, although easily quashed, became a symbol of resistance to oppression, and the educated public never forgave the government for the brutal reprisals against the insurgents.

Nicholas I, a stern and unimaginative military man, was obsessed by the goals of stamping out all dissent and inculcating his official "ideology" of autocracy, Orthodoxy, and Russian nationalism. He established the notorious Third Department of the Chancery, whose secret police were empowered to investigate "all occurrences without exception." Censorship became so pervasive that a book on ancient history was not permitted to mention that the Roman emperors had been murdered, and musical scores were inspected on the suspicion that they might contain subversive messages in code.

Czarist repression could not stifle what was destined to be a brilliant period in Russian literature. The young Aleksandr Pushkin—who supported the Decembrists but escaped punishment because he was already in exile for penning revolutionary epigrams—produced masterpieces of prose and poetry that helped Russian literature find its voice. Works such as *Eugene Onegin* and *The Bronze Horseman* established themes that would be explored by Russian writers for decades, from the alienation of the educated gentry to the tragic consequences of Peter the Great's modernizing reforms for the common man. Perhaps more important, Pushkin's mastery of many

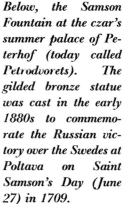

Below, the Samson Fountain at the czar's summer palace of Peterhof (today called Petrodvorets). The gilded bronze statue was cast in the early 1880s to commemorate the Russian victory over the Swedes at Poltava on Saint Samson's Day (June 27) in 1709.

genres provided his heirs with great models of literary Russian. After Pushkin, no censor could destroy the conviction among Russian writers that they were working in a tradition staked out by an artist of world stature.

At a time when every new idea carried with it a whiff of subversion, literature was bound to have a political impact. The works of Nikolai Gogol are a case in point. One of Gogol's best-known plays, *The Inspector General,* dealt with a braggart clerk who is mistaken for a government inspector traveling incognito and plied with bribes and favors by corrupt local officials. That stern censor Nicholas I approved the text, apparently interpreting it as straightforward slapstick, yet the drama was widely received as a stinging satire on the venality and backwardness of provincial life.

Left, the retreating French at the city of Smolensk. Above, a Russian division giving chase to French cavalrymen.

1812: The peasants against the foreigner

When Napoleon launched his invasion of Russia in 1812, he did not expect to meet strong resistance, either from the notoriously irresolute Alexander I or from the oppressed peasantry. To Napoleon's surprise, Russians from the czar on down—convinced that the French emperor was Antichrist who had come to violate Holy Russia—refused to even consider submitting to surrender. Regular army units performed admirably, peasants burned their crops rather than leave them behind to feed the Grande Armée, and Cossack and peasant partisans mercilessly attacked stragglers from the French forces.

No doubt many Russians acted from motives other than patriotism. Some peasants were simply trying to save themselves from the horde of desperate, half-starved soldiers. Others were inflamed by propaganda claiming that Napoleon meant to close the churches and force Russians to worship him as a god. Nevertheless, revulsion against the invaders did briefly unite all classes in a common cause.

The general euphoria produced by Russia's victory was punctured by the czar's admonition that the serfs should expect their reward only "from God." Not all veterans of 1812 were so ungrateful, however. For many of the gentry, the peasants would never again be an invisible class.

Below, two allegorical prints showing French soldiers captured by peasants (left) and several of Napoleon's generals retreating in a Russian sleigh (right).

Right, three prints representing the peasants' role in the struggle against Napoleon (top to bottom): a peasant woman shutting French soldiers inside an izba, a peasant taking a cannon from the French, and a group of peasants locking terrified Frenchmen inside a house.

Eventually, the very term "intelligentsia," which designated the entire educated class, came to be synonymous with antigovernment protest. At the conservative end of the spectrum were the Slavophiles, who viewed all of Russian history from the time of Peter the Great as a deviation from the unique mission of Slavic culture and Orthodox religion. Despite their opposition to Western-style constitutional government, the Slavophiles were distrusted by the regime because they favored emancipation of the serfs and were harshly critical of the bureaucratic state. The Slavophiles' opponents, the Westernizers, were by no means a unified school. They ranged from liberals favoring a very gradual transition to constitutional rule to the young Aleksandr Herzen, who claimed to have found in Hegel a blueprint for revolution. Herzen, who lived most of his life in exile, later became disillusioned by the failures and hypocrisy of western European liberalism and came to see Russia's salvation in socialism based on egalitarian peasant communes. Herzen distrusted violence—he once wrote that what Russia needed was not an ax but a broom—but his contemporary Mikhail Bakunin took an active part in the European revolutions of 1848–1849 and proclaimed the anarchist doctrine that "the business of revolutionaries is to destroy the State in order to free the people."

The social criticism of the intelligentsia was underscored by the dismaying experience of the Crimean War of 1853–1856. Thinking the Ottoman Empire moribund, Nicholas had begun to anticipate a partition of Turkish lands. Nicholas believed he had the tacit support of the British, but he had not counted on the apprehension that would be aroused throughout Europe by his invasion of Turkish provinces in present-day Romania, ostensibly in defense of the Orthodox Christian population. By the autumn of 1854, a joint Turkish, British, French, and Sardinian fleet had besieged the Russian fortress of Sevastopol in the Crimea. Once again, Russian soldiers fought bravely—their ranks reinforced by serfs who joined the army after hearing rumors that volunteers would be granted their freedom—but the rest of the war effort, from the performance of the general staff to the mobilization of the civilian economy, proved inadequate to the occasion. Sevastopol's surrender in September 1855 greatly diminished Russia's prestige abroad and convinced many of the czar's subjects that serfdom stood in the way of economic modernization and military revival.

Indeed, some landlords had already discovered that serf labor and modern farming methods were not a profitable combination. Alexander II, who became emperor following the death of his father, Nicholas,

Facing page, the burning of Moscow in September 1812. The cause of the fire has been vigorously debated. Most historians believe the city was torched by the departing Russian governor after the French entered the city.

Left, Aleksandr Suvorov, the Russian army commander who won a series of celebrated victories against the French in the late eighteenth century. Below, Napoleon's Grand Armée retreating in panic across a river in November 1812.

Above, a nineteenth-century izba, or country house, of the type built by prosperous peasant families.

Below, peasants at a cockfight. This form of entertainment was widespread throughout the Russian Empire.

The peasant commune

Even in the early twentieth century, Russia was still very much a rural country. Three quarters of the population were peasants, and ties to the home village remained strong among those who had migrated to the towns to work in industry. Although many provincial districts were seriously overpopulated, the peasant commune system discouraged young people from leaving home; a family was threatened with a reduction in its land allotment, for example, if a family member abandoned the commune.

The commune in time came to be dismissed as an anachronism by liberals and Marxists. Land reforms undertaken after 1905 made it easier for wealthier peasants to consolidate their landholdings and leave the commune. Nonetheless, the basic imbalance between the poor, who paid the lion's share of all taxes, and the gentry, who owned more land than they could put to use, was never resolved.

Above, a festive gathering of relatives and friends at a peasant wedding. A foreign observer once remarked: "The arrival of a daughter-in-law, even the poorest, is a reason for celebration: She brings another pair of hands to work, and her sons, right from birth, are assigned a piece of land [from the peasant commune]."

Left, the interior of a peasant home. Right, a peasant's home with a loft sleeping platform. Only the larger houses were divided into several rooms; most peasant dwellings had one room—and even that meager space was sometimes shared by fowls, goats, and other small animals. The typical peasant's home had only a few pieces of wooden furniture. A large stove heated the house in winter; on especially cold nights the children slept on a thick wooden board placed above the stove.

The lion (above) and spiral foliage patterns (below) are among the most ancient and popular motifs used by peasant woodcarvers.

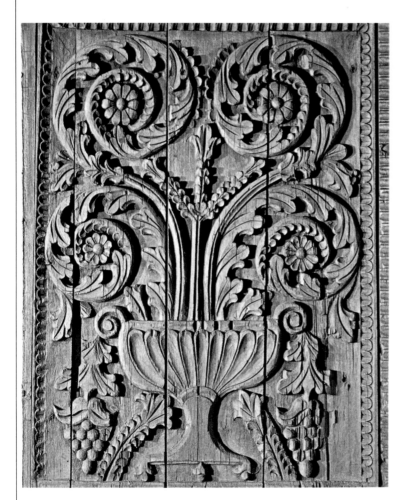

The art of woodcarving

Until the time of Peter the Great, even the wealthiest aristocratic families lived surrounded by the work of peasant woodcarvers. Rustic furniture, ornate interior woodwork, and elaborately carved wooden serving vessels and utensils with various popular motifs were fashionable until the eighteenth century, when the gentry began to favor Western-style furnishings, either imported or impeccably copied by highly skilled serf craftsmen. There was still a great demand for traditional woodcraft, especially in the outlying countryside, but the preferences of gentry employers and the influence of industrialization eventually threatened its survival. During the last decades of the empire, the craft of the peasant woodcarver was revitalized thanks to the continuing efforts of wealthy Slavophile patrons, who sponsored workshops in an attempt to keep peasant art forms alive.

These decorative extensions on the eaves of a wooden house (left) recall the highly stylized Russian roof ornaments of medieval times. Above and below left, carvings from the Volga region. Right and below, decorative borders carved in high relief.

in 1855, summed up the situation realistically when he warned that it would be better to abolish serfdom from above than to wait for it to abolish itself from below. On March 3, 1861, the emperor signed a proclamation emancipating the serfs. The "Era of the Great Reforms" had begun.

It was one thing to abolish serfdom with a stroke of the pen and another to undo the consequences of a system centuries in the making. The emancipation plan called for landlords to be compensated for land transferred to the peasant communes, to which the serfs remained bound. The amount of land allotted the communes was often insufficient, and the redemption payments were so onerous that most villagers soon fell into debt.

In spite of the shortcomings of the emancipation settlement, the decade of the 1860s was one of prom-

"As for Nicholas, he has but one ambition—to reign." This blunt appraisal of Nicholas I (above left) was penned by the czar's own mother.

Above, Cathedral Square in the Kremlin as it was during the nineteenth century. Right, assorted depictions of Russians at the time of Nicholas I. The knout (near right) was a leather whip used to flog criminals.

ising changes. Alexander's other great reforms included the establishment of an independent judiciary and the creation of zemstvos, or local assemblies, which encouraged at least limited participation in government affairs. But the emperor's ministers hoped to preserve the autocracy by controlling the pace of reform, and by the second half of the decade they nervously began to apply the brakes.

To the new generation of the intelligentsia, this piecemeal doling out of reform from above was insufferable. The students of the 1860s represented a broader spectrum of Russian society—they were the sons and daughters of physicians, shopkeepers, and peasants—and they were angrier and more impatient than their predecessors of the 1840s. Among them were the youthful firebrands whom the novelist Ivan Turgenev called nihilists. They preferred to think of themselves as "new men."

The nihilism of the 1860s was essentially a period of self-assertion. The radicals of the next decade became acutely aware of the gap between themselves and the great masses of the Russian people. In the spring of 1874, several thousand students went "to the people," that is, to provincial towns and villages. Some became village doctors, teachers, and agricultural experts; a few were willing to listen and learn while they proselytized; many naively believed that they could distribute a handful of pamphlets, make fiery speeches, and inspire the benighted peasants to revolutionary action. So confident were these populist crusaders that they made little attempt to hide their activities from the czarist police. The peasants, meanwhile, proved more suspicious and less pliant than the radicals had imagined. Within a few months, many of the radicals were in jail, some denounced by the very peasants they had planned to liberate.

The collapse of the movement "to the people" left the populists demoralized, and a dedicated few concluded that the only recourse was a program of terrorism and assassination. One secret society, The People's Will, set out to kill the emperor himself. This was a formidable task for the tiny group of conspirators, whose active members were seldom more than a step away from arrest. On one occasion, the society blew up the dining room of the Winter Palace, killing eleven people, only to discover that Alexander was absent at the time of the explosion. Again, they dynamited a train—but not, it happened, the emperor's. Finally, on March 13, 1881, the terrorists succeeded in killing Alexander, the czar-liberator, with a bomb thrown at his open carriage.

In 1855, after blundering into the Crimean War, Nicholas I died, leaving his son to cope with the consequences of the fall of the Crimean fortress of Sevastopol (right). This fanciful scene (below right) shows Queen Victoria of Britain, Napoleon III of France, and a Turkish plenipotentiary presenting the terms of the Treaty of Paris to Alexander II.

Above, an 1868 painting of the czarina and her entourage on a pilgrimage to a monastery near Moscow. Right, a gold five-rouble piece and a silver twenty-kopeck piece. Paper money (left) was just winning acceptance among the peasants in the mid-nineteenth century.

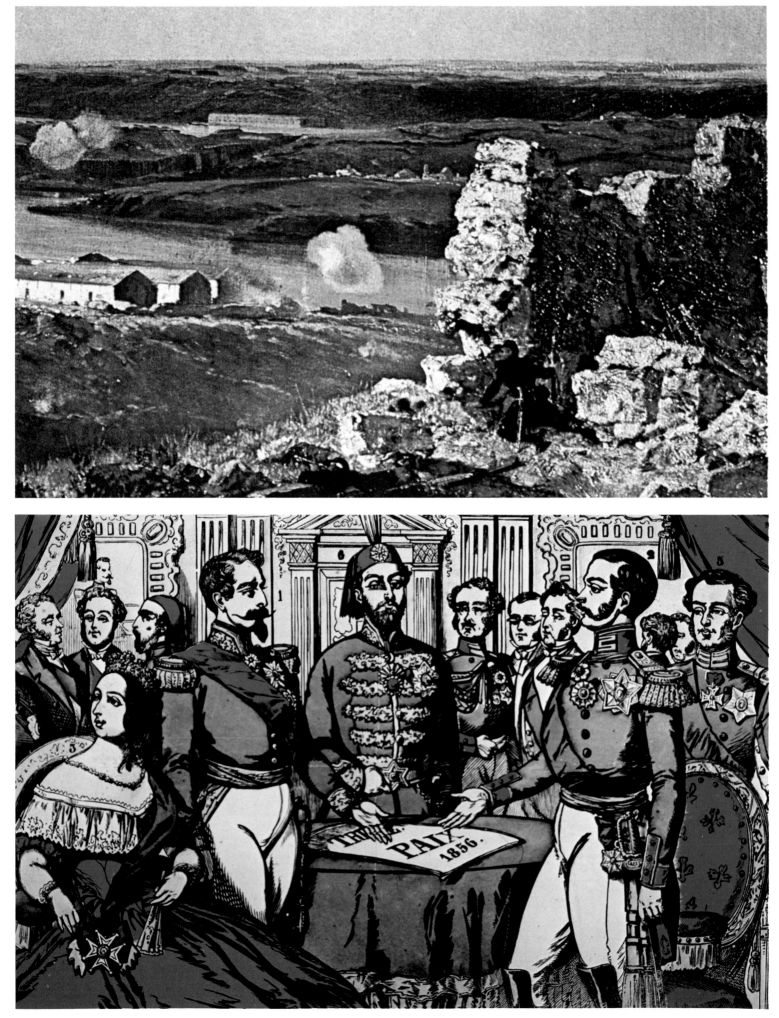

In the nineteenth century, Russia actively attempted to consolidate its hold on Siberia. Kamchatka was re-explored, and Yakutsk (immediately below) on the Lena River grew from a fur-trading post into the world's northernmost agricultural center. Left, a peasant's hut in Kamchatka.

Lower left, the Tela Kori mosque in Samarkand, a city annexed by Russia in 1868. Parts of Armenia, a nation with ancient cultural traditions, were annexed by the empire in the eighteenth century. Lower right, a monastery complex overlooking Armenia's Lake Sevan.

The People's Will had hoped that its desperate actions would accomplish one of two goals: Either the government would be intimidated into stepping up the pace of reform or the people would be inspired to mass revolution. Neither of these objectives was realized. The new emperor, Alexander III, was cast in the mold of his grandfather Nicholas, and his ministers were quite candid about their desire to turn back the clock—one official even considered measures to "keep people from inventing things." In addition, Alexander's government actively persecuted religious minorities and all subjects who were not ethnic Great Russians. The Jews, always suspect in the eyes of the

Orthodox Church, were for the most part confined to the districts known collectively as the Pale of Jewish Settlement, and 1881 saw the first of many pogroms.

Imperial Russia's last half-century was a dynamic era, but one permeated by growing social tension. The country became a major exporter of grain to world markets thanks to the development of steam-powered ocean transport and the adoption of modern farming methods by some landlords. By 1890 unmistakable signs of an industrial revolution had appeared. Russian capitalists and foreign investors grew rich by tapping the country's vast natural resources,

building factories, and extending the railroad network into Siberia and central Asia. The rapid growth of capitalism, however, only widened the gap between the rich and the poor. St. Petersburg society remained a shimmering round of balls and entertainments, dominated by the nouveaux riches and great families like the Yusupovs, who could serve two thousand guests from Sèvres china and gold-plated vessels. In the same city an industrial working class, miserably housed and ill-paid, was growing restive. Radical youths, many of gentry or middle-class origin, were increasingly attracted to Marxism as an alternative to populism's romantic glorification of the backward peasant commune.

Stimulated by intellectual and political ferment, Russian culture of this period captured the world's attention. Lev Tolstoi's epic novel *War and Peace* and Modest Moussorgsky's *Boris Godunov*, both products of Alexander II's times, recalled vanished eras of Russian history. The spirit of the Era of the Great Reforms was penetratingly examined in Tolstoi's *Anna Karenina* and in the great realistic novels of Fyodor Dostoyevsky and Turgenev. At the turn of the century, Anton Chekhov's stories and plays hauntingly evoked the nostalgia and frustration of the provincial gentry and middle class, and Maxim Gorki depicted

The opening of Siberia proceeded apace in the early years of the twentieth century, encouraged by the completion of the Trans-Siberian Railroad and agricultural reforms enabling more peasants to settle on the eastern frontier. Mile-deep Lake Baikal (above) contains ten percent of the world's freshwater resources. Below, Siberian flora and fauna.

Alexander III (left) was described by one of his ministers as "just another Peter the Great with a cudgel." "Not at all," replied a second minister. "He is just the cudgel without Peter the Great attached." Facing page, above, an 1881 painting of Peter's bloody suppression of the streltsy (palace guard) in 1698—an indirect condemnation of reactionary nineteenth-century czars. Facing page, below, an 1885 painting that is a more forthright protest against the jailing of dissidents.

with moving pathos the plight of Russia's downtrodden. Symbolism and "modernism"—movements that reflected the international art nouveau style—were vehicles for a brilliant outburst of experimentation in literature, music, and painting. Konstantin Stanislavsky's Moscow Art Theater, the Imperial Russian Ballet of St. Petersburg, Sergei Diaghilev's Ballets Russes, and such luminous performers as Anna Pavlova, Vaslav Nijinsky, and Fyodor Chaliapin set world standards in the arts.

The Russian Empire of the late nineteenth century was drawing closer to Europe economically and culturally, but its geographic center was in Asia—a fact that was beginning to stir the imagination of Russian policy makers. Ever since the time of Ivan the Terrible, Russians had been engaged in the exploration and settlement of the eastern frontier, an epic undertaking comparable with the opening of the American West. The first Russians in Siberia were hardy Cossack fur traders. As early as 1639 a band of Cossacks reached the Pacific Ocean, and by the 1690s Russians occupied the Kamchatka peninsula in eastern Siberia and established a border with China that would remain fixed for almost two centuries. Since furs were crucial to Russia's foreign trade, the government in Moscow had taken a strong interest in these activities, acting as the principal broker for the traders and forcing indigenous Siberian peoples to pay a tax in fur pelts.

Hoping to discover an Arctic sea route linking European Russia to the Far East, Peter the Great commissioned an expedition by the Dane Vitus Bering. Bering's first voyage in 1728 was disappointing, but on his second, thirteen years later, the crew landed in Alaska. In the meantime, the Siberian exploration project had been placed under the auspices of the Academy of Sciences, which invited foreign naturalists, geologists, and ethnographers to participate. These efforts added greatly to knowledge of Siberia and its resources but touched off rebellions among the inhabitants of Kamchatka, who were pressed into service by the Russians.

Above, a stage setting for the second act of the Imperial Russian Ballet's production of The Sleeping Beauty. *Right, a costume sketch for the ballet* Puss in Boots.

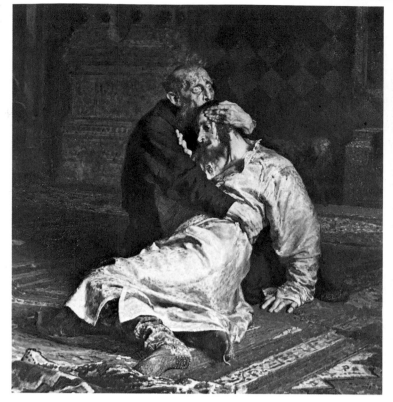

Left, Repin's portrait of Sophia, Peter the Great's half sister. Above, Ivan the Terrible remorsefully embracing his murdered son Ivan.

The Volga Boatmen (above) became one of Repin's most popular works. Left, a painting of the novelist Lev Tolstoi working as a plowman on his large country estate.

This exuberant painting entitled Zaporozhye Cossacks Writing a Letter to the Turkish Sultan *(right) recalls the Ukrainian Cossacks' rebuke of a Turkish annexation attempt in 1671. Immediately below, a detail of a portrait of Lev Tolstoi. Bottom,* Religious Procession in Kursk Gubernia.

Ilya Repin

Born in 1844, Ilya Repin came to maturity at a time when Russian artists were striving to give their work social relevance. In 1863 thirteen painters resigned from the Russian Academy rather than submit works on the theme chosen for the annual competition—the banquet of the gods at Valhalla. This group later formed the Society of Wandering Exhibitions, or the Wanderers, to promote art advocating social reform. Although Repin never formally joined the Wanderers, he was greatly influenced by their philosophy for much of his career. At the time of his death in 1930, Repin had gained a wide reputation for his portraits of famous contemporaries, his numerous historical paintings, and his realistic studies of ordinary people at work.

By the nineteenth century, Russian fur-trading posts stretched along the coast of Alaska and as far south as Fort Ross in California. The mining of copper and silver became a major industry in the interior of Siberia. The population of Russian colonists expanded as peasants who had moved to escape the gentry-dominated economy in the west were joined by members of the intelligentsia, banished in large numbers during the reign of Nicholas I.

After Nicholas' death in 1855, Russia began to regard itself as a major power in Asia. In the second half of the nineteenth century, when Alaska was sold to the United States and all Russian claims to the Western Hemisphere surrendered, the Russians invaded and conquered central Asia, pushed the border with China southward, and founded a number of towns—notably Vladivostok and Khabarovsk—on the Pacific coast. In 1891, three years before Nicholas II's accession, work commenced on the Trans-Siberian Railroad, a project that would make it possible to tap Siberia's wealth to an extent never before envisioned.

In 1894, Alexander III died, and his son Nicholas II ascended the throne—woefully ill prepared by his overbearing father for the tasks before him. Determined to preserve autocracy and extend Russia's

Above, Nicholas II and Empress Alexandra, formerly Princess Alix of Hesse-Darmstadt, at the time of their marriage in 1894. Despite the efforts of Kaiser William II of Germany (below, with arms akimbo), Russia became allied with France. Right, Nicholas in Paris.

borders, Nicholas listened to the worst possible advisers. In 1904 his attempt to assert Russian domination over Manchuria and Korea led to a brief and disastrous war with Japan. Domestic opposition to the conflict mounted, and on January 22, 1905, the day known as Bloody Sunday, nervous police opened fire on a group of peaceful demonstraters as they converged on St. Petersburg's Winter Palace to petition the czar for peace and bread. The bloodshed shattered forever the ordinary Russians' faith in the czar as their benevolent "little father," and throughout 1905 the country was convulsed by increasingly violent urban riots, rural uprisings, and naval mutinies.

Finally, in October 1905, having made peace with Japan through the mediation of President Theodore Roosevelt, Nicholas was forced by a general strike to permit the election of a representative assembly, the Duma, to assist in carrying out fundamental political reforms. A century after Speranski's proposals to Alexander I, Russia again seemed on the verge of becoming a constitutional monarchy.

The first Duma convened in May 1906 in an atmosphere of optimism. The Cadets, a moderate liberal party, dominated the assembly, and one English observer commented approvingly on the dignity and order of the Duma's proceedings, predicting that "the

Nicholas' attempt to make Russia a dominant power in Asia led to a disastrous war with Japan. The naval battle of Port Arthur (above), off the Chinese coast, and the Japanese occupation of Sakhalin Island (right) were episodes in a conflict finally resolved through the mediation of President Theodore Roosevelt.

Duma will soon learn to be as disorderly as the House of Commons." It soon became evident, however, that Nicholas and his ministers had no intention of allowing the Duma to control the government. The first Duma was dismissed after seventy-three days. The second, in which Vladimir Ilyich Lenin's left-wing Bolsheviks and the parties of the extreme right gained substantial ground, was also dismissed. A third Duma managed to serve out its full five-year term only because it had been elected under a new law ensuring that half of its members would be chosen by the gentry.

A promising development of this period was the launching of a long overdue program of agrarian reform to lift the burden of redemption payments from the peasant communes and permit peasants to settle in Siberia. This plan, enacted by the third Duma, was adopted at the urging of Nicholas' talented prime minister, Pëtr Stolypin. But in 1911, before he could carry out other planned reforms, Stolypin was assassinated by the czar's own secret police, who feared his growing power.

Even Nicholas' better impulses, arising from his devotion to his wife and family, had ruinous consequences. Concerned for the health of his hemophiliac son, Alexis, Nicholas permitted the czarina Alexandra to become dependent on a bizarre faith healer and "holy man," Grigori Rasputin. If Rasputin was a hypnotist, as contemporary accounts suggest, he may indeed have saved Alexis' life on occasion. (Present-day experiments with hypnotism as a means of controlling hemophiliac bleeding were inspired by descriptions of Rasputin's successes.) Overcome by gratitude, the imperial couple failed to heed warnings about Rasputin's trafficking in favors and scandalous behavior with women of all classes.

Russia's entry into World War One in June 1914 appeared at first to unite czar and people in a common cause. The decision to declare war on Austria-Hungary (an ally of Germany) in support of Serbia was a logical outcome of Russia's interest in the Balkans; however, the Russian people soon realized that the hard lessons of the past were due to be repeated. Although the front-line troops performed heroically, the government was unable to mobilize the economy and the transport system. By 1915, Russian officers were sending unarmed troops into battle, instructing soldiers to scavenge weapons from fallen comrades. To make matters worse, Nicholas insisted on going to the front, where he served no purpose—leaving the czarina and Rasputin to meddle unchecked in government business.

The collapse of the Romanov dynasty was not so much a consequence of the Russian revolution as a

Above, imperial soldiers charging demonstrators on "Bloody Sunday" in 1905. Below, peasants and workers meeting on the outskirts of Moscow. Right, the spirit of the 1905 revolt is recalled in a Bolshevik poster: "The 1905 revolution has united the workers and Lenin in the gunpowder's smoke."

РАБОЧИХ и ЛЕНИНА
СОЕДИНИЛА В СВОЕМ ПОРОХОВОМ
ДЫМУ

РЕВОЛЮЦИЯ 1905 г.

prelude to it. By 1916 even intimates of the royal family saw the necessity of change and resorted to desperate measures. A band of conspirators, led by Prince Feliks Yusupov, husband of the czar's niece, assassinated the hated Rasputin. The deed removed the symbol of the family's degeneracy but did little to restore faith in Nicholas' rule. In February 1917, St. Petersburg (renamed Petrograd as an anti-German gesture) was swept by demonstrations protesting extreme shortages of bread and coal. By this time even the monarchists in the Duma agreed that Nicholas would have to go, and on March 15, after a week of turmoil in the streets and mutinies among the imperial guards, Nicholas signed an abdication agreement passing over his invalid son, Alexis, in favor of his brother, Michael.

Legend had it that when the second Michael Romanov sat on the Russian throne the empire would conquer Constantinople at last. Ironically, England and France had promised Constantinople to Russia as an inducement to stay in the war, but the symbolic relationship between Russia and Byzantium, which had once served the purposes of Ivan the Great so well, now stood for something quite different in the minds of most Russians—an outmoded, autocratic regime and a disastrous European war. Michael II had reigned only twenty-four hours before he hastily renounced his claim to the throne. One month later, Lenin arrived home from exile in Switzerland, determined that the collapse of the autocracy would be only the first step toward a socialist revolution.

Portugal of the Navigators

The Portuguese were the vanguard of colonialism, the first Western people to be impelled by the restless spirit of expansionism into Africa, Asia, and South America. Portugal's navigators were the first Europeans to career down the Atlantic coast of Africa and around the Cape of Good Hope, thereby opening the Indian Ocean to the ships of the West. Moving swiftly to exploit the breakthroughs in exploration, Portuguese traders reached the shores of Japan in 1543, just fifty-five years after Bartholomeu Dias rounded the south African cape.

Their enterprise won the Portuguese a rich and

Preceding page, a Portuguese fleet as depicted in a sixteenth-century miniature. Farms amidst Portugal's rolling hills (above) produce grain, grapes, and olives. Below, a windmill for grinding grain along the Atlantic coast.

varied trade, and an empire embracing three continents. From Brazil to Japan, stately cargo vessels called carracks voyaged to distant ports to gather exotic goods—from pepper to porcelain—for the warehouses of Lisbon.

Paradoxically, Portugal's flourishing trade never really enriched the basically agricultural homeland, whose industrial and cultural achievements lagged far behind those of other countries. The nation was unable to escape indebtedness to foreign creditors, while its conservative nobility thwarted the aspirations of Portugal's own small middle class. Scarcity of both money and manpower prevented Portugal from

developing a strong military elite, with the result that more vigorous countries, notably England and Holland, eventually seized the Asian harvests that Portugal had sown.

Yet despite world wars and political upheavals at home, Portugal managed to cling to some of its colonies well into the twentieth century. Until the 1960s Portugal still had a foothold in India; until the 1970s large regions of Africa still flew the Portuguese flag. The first European empire lived to be the last.

The Portuguese are descended from many ancient peoples. In the first millennium before Christ, the

Portugal's rocky shoreline sheltered smugglers and provided numerous inlets that harbored fishing boats. Above, Estoril, and left, the Point of Stones, two promontories along the coast. Below, the Douro River.

northern and central regions of present-day Portugal were inhabited by Celtic tribes and the southern coastline by Greek and Carthaginian fishermen. The Romans conquered much of the Iberian Peninsula in the second century B.C., imposing their customs and language on the inhabitants—modern Portuguese and Spanish derive from the Latin dialect spoken on the peninsula during the Roman occupation.

Teutonic, or Germanic, Visigoths swept into Iberia in the fifth century A.D. and ruled until the Moors— Moslems from North Africa—invaded their kingdom in 711. Within two years the southern half of the peninsula was under Moorish control. The defeated Visigoths rallied in the north where they established small Christian kingdoms and began the herculean task of ousting the Moors. This period is known as the Reconquest. One of these kingdoms—composed of the states of León and Castile—included the county of Portugal, bounded roughly by the Atlantic on the west, the mouths of the Minho and Mondego rivers on the north and south, and Portugal's present border on the east.

Late in the eleventh century, King Alfonso of León and Castile gave dominion over this county to Henry, a knight from Burgundy, in exchange for his help against the Moors. In 1139, Henry's son, Afonso

Before Portugal's oldest university was permanently established at Coimbra in 1537, medieval Portugal's most important centers of learning were monasteries. Above, a monk at his writing table, from an eleventh-century miniature.

Left, a scene of a vineyard and winepress of the twelfth century, drawn by a Benedictine monk at the monastery of Lorvão. Wine making has been an important industry throughout Portugal's history.

Henriques, became king of the independent state of Portugal, as Alfonso I. Alfonso and his successors gradually enlarged the nation, pushing the Moors farther and farther south until the boundaries of what is present-day Portugal were reached around 1250.

In 1279, King Diniz, perhaps the greatest of the medieval Portuguese monarchs, came to power and set out to improve Portugal's emerging navy. He invited a Genoese sea captain to Portugal, gave him the title of admiral, and placed him in charge of developing the mercantile and naval fleets. In 1341, under Alfonso IV, a fleet of three vessels, commanded by Italian captains, sailed from Lisbon and explored the Canary Islands, off the northwestern coast of Africa. Though the expedition showed no profit and Castile later succeeded in gaining control of the islands, this voyage was the first official exploring expedition by a European state.

From the time that Portugal had attained its autonomy, it was forced to contend with the repeated attempts of Castile to retake its breakaway county. This conflict culminated in the 1385 battle of Aljubarrota, during which the army of the Portuguese king John I, aided by English archers, defeated a Castilian invasion force and ensured Portugal's independence. No less important, John founded the royal dynasty of Aviz, which presided over the great era of Portuguese discovery—an era that was launched by his son Prince Henry, known as the Navigator.

Though Portugal had freed itself from Moorish rule over a century before John ascended the throne in 1385, the effects of the struggle were still being felt. The long period of the Reconquest had been a formative one for the Portuguese national character: It instilled an underlying hostility toward all adherents of Islam regardless of race or nationality as well as an enduring crusading zeal. It was missionary fervor, in large part, that spirited the Portuguese on explorations whose purpose was to reduce the power of Islam and convert nonbelievers to the Christian faith. Within this plan lay the goal of locating the Christian kingdom of Prester John—a mythical monarch who ruled, according to European belief, over a fabulously wealthy and powerful kingdom somewhere in Asia or Africa. He supposedly commanded an army of four and a half million men and routinely feasted thirty thousand guests at his emerald dinner table, where twelve archbishops sat at his right hand and twenty bishops at his left. The Portuguese hoped to enlist his help in a worldwide crusade against Islam.

Moslem dominance of the world's commerce in the two most valued commodities—spices and gold—

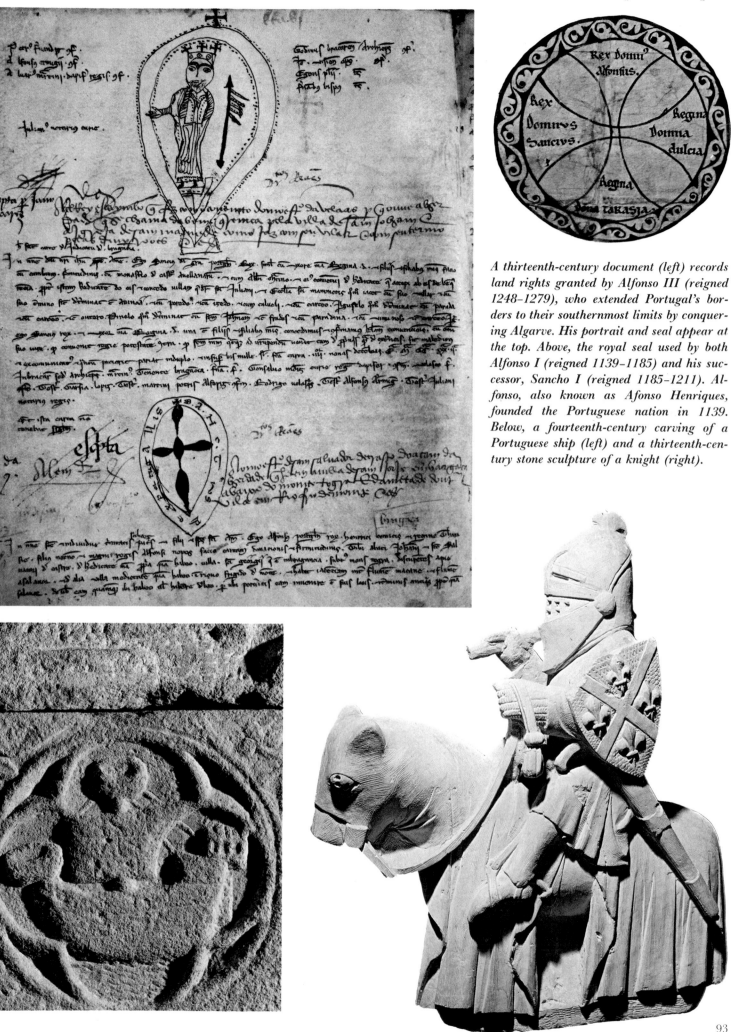

A thirteenth-century document (left) records land rights granted by Alfonso III (reigned 1248–1279), who extended Portugal's borders to their southernmost limits by conquering Algarve. His portrait and seal appear at the top. Above, the royal seal used by both Alfonso I (reigned 1139–1185) and his successor, Sancho I (reigned 1185–1211). Alfonso, also known as Afonso Henriques, founded the Portuguese nation in 1139. Below, a fourteenth-century carving of a Portuguese ship (left) and a thirteenth-century stone sculpture of a knight (right).

added a further economic incentive to the Portuguese crusade. In the 1400s, Europe was suffering a gold shortage, which drove up the value of the metal one thousand percent in less than fifty years. The Portuguese had only a vague sense of where the metal came from: It originated in mines somewhere in Africa, then found its way to the West African trading city of Timbuktu, where it was carried off by Moslem merchants to their markets. Moslems in Asia and Egypt also controlled the shipment of spices from the Indies (later known as the East Indies)—India, Southeast Asia, and the Malay Archipelago—to the Egyptian seaport of Alexandria. Here, the precious cargoes were bought by Venetian traders,who commanded a monopoly on the European spice market.

Spices were more a necessity than a luxury to the Europeans. During the long winters they were ob-

liged to eat meat from animals that had been slaughtered in the fall. Much of this meat was virtually spoiled by the time it was consumed, and spices, especially pepper, were in great demand to disguise the taste and smell. Prices for this essential commodity naturally were high, and the Portuguese hoped to find their own route to the Indies to break the Venetian stranglehold.

The Portuguese conjectured that the solution could be found by sailing around Africa, but they had no idea of the size or even the shape of the continent. In fact, maps produced by the famed second-century geographer Ptolemy, although a thousand years old, were still in use. Showing southern Africa solidly connected with Asia and the route to the Indian Ocean blocked off, these maps were considered the true picture of the world by many scholars of the time. Ac-

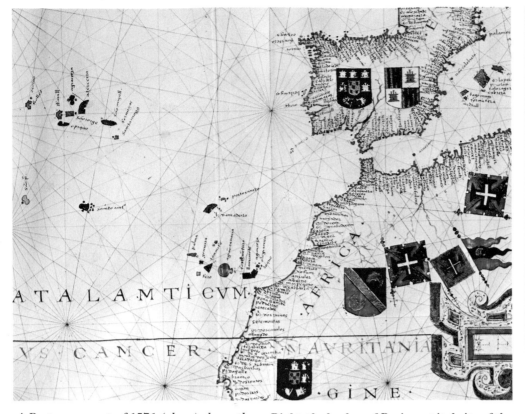

A Portuguese map of 1571 (above) shows the location of the Azores and Madeira, which remain part of Portugal to this day, and the Canary Islands, which were ceded to Castile by treaty in 1479.

Right, the harbor of Praia, capital city of the Cape Verde Islands, as depicted in a seventeenth-century Dutch painting. Located on the island of São Tiago, the city supports a European population.

cording to some geographers the best hope of entering the Indian Ocean was to trace a river that flowed through southern Africa into that body of water. But even if a route to the Indian Ocean could be found, the Green Sea of Darkness—an uncrossable sea of violent storms and impenetrable mist that, the Arabs declared lay off the coast of western Africa—was another persistent obstacle to a route to the Indies.

Because of their ignorance of the immense size of the African continent, the Portuguese of Prince Henry's time were obsessed with the desire to conquer Morocco, in North Africa, which they saw as a stepping stone to control of the gold trade. Despite the opposition of the ever-cautious King John, Prince Henry and a "war party" of nobles, who were as intent on winning personal glory as on carrying out a rational plan of expansion, laid plans for an assault on the Moroccan trading port of Ceuta. The king was finally persuaded to approve the project, and a fleet of some two hundred vessels landed troops outside the walls of the city. Ceuta fell to the Portuguese in 1415 after one day of fighting. It was an easy victory that yielded abundant spoils to the conquerors, but no lasting military or financial advantage.

Though modern historians have dwelt upon Henry's misadventures in Morocco and even have

questioned the appropriateness of calling him the Navigator in view of his having ventured no farther than Tangier, the fact remains that Henry set Portugal on its course toward overseas expansion. Indeed, one of his most famous accomplishments was the establishment of a center for the study of navigation, naval architecture, and astronomy at Sagres in southern Portugal.

The Portuguese learned much about navigation from two peoples they actively persecuted—the Moors and the Jews; ironically, the contributions of these groups never tempered Portuguese enmity. Specifically, the Portuguese navigators were deeply indebted to the Jews for their profound knowledge of astronomy and mathematics. Jewish astrologers had carefully plotted the positions of the stars, and were soon to combine this knowledge with mathematics to advance the craft of navigating by the heavens. The Moors, meanwhile, had developed navigational instruments like the quadrant, astrolabe, and compass, with the knowledge of these developments coming to the Portuguese directly from Moorish Spain and indirectly through Jewish merchants trading with the Arabs. Of equal importance was the development of the ship called the caravel. Under Henry's guidance the Portuguese adopted and improved the design of

Top, the shore of São Tiago, largest of the Cape Verde Islands. The islands are mainly agricultural, producing coffee, sugar cane, bananas, and tobacco. Immediately above, the mountainous interior of the island of Madeira.

Left, terraced fields on the east coast of Santa Maria, an island in the Azores archipelago. The Azores and Madeira were Portugal's first colonies, with Portuguese settlers arriving there in the fifteenth century. The colonies' farms provided much-needed wheat to the motherland and served as ports-of-call for voyages of exploration.

97

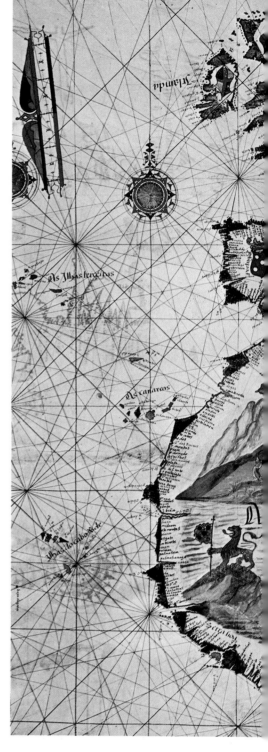

Above, a portion of the will of Prince Ferdinand (1402–1443), who was captured in battle in Morocco and died in a Moorish prison. Below, a map of Africa based on Ptolemy's second-century Geography. *Right, a more accurate mid-sixteenth-century map of the African continent.*

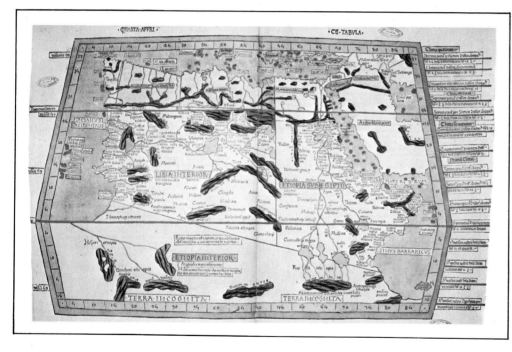

the caravel, whose chief advantage over the older Portuguese ships was its triangular, "lateen" sail, which could be trimmed to allow the ship to proceed in either cross or head winds.

Soon after the victory at Ceuta, Prince Henry began dispatching ships into the Atlantic with orders to proceed as far as possible, map the coast or any islands sighted, and return. His program brought almost immediate results, when one of his captains rediscovered the islands of Madeira and the Azores—first scouted by King Diniz's Genoese admiral. Henry ordered his captains to continue south, but the horror stories about the Green Sea of Darkness, concocted by

the Arabs to deter Christian explorers, began to have their intended effect. Portuguese mariners approaching Cape Bojador, on the northwestern coast of Africa, repeatedly turned back as they ran into the thick fog and high seas that are still known to afflict mariners there. The Arabs claimed that beyond this cape boiling seas produced an intense heat which no man could survive—this fiction made the cape as much a psychological obstacle as a physical one. It is said that the prince ordered one of his most trusted captains, Gil Eanes, to round the cape at any cost and that Eanes turned back fifteen times before finally passing it in 1433.

Right, a stone circle at Sagres. With over forty lines radiating from its center, it is believed by some to have served as a compass. Below, the Portuguese army in Morocco in 1471, just before its assault on Tangier and Arzila.

Within a decade after Eanes' breakthrough, Prince Henry's ships began to bring gold dust and slaves back from the African coast. In 1445 the Portuguese established a "factory," or trading station, on the island of Arguin, several hundred miles south of Cape Bojador, to gather gold, slaves, and ivory. This gold trade was so successful that by 1457, after a lapse of some seventy-four years, during which time gold had been unavailable in Portugal, Alfonso V was able to resume minting gold coins. The new coin was called, significantly, the cruzado, or crusade, pointing to the mixture of commercial and religious motives behind Portugal's overseas expansion.

This mingling of motives became even more obvious in that same decade when the Crown sought papal blessing for its enterprises, as well as a Church-approved monopoly on the African trade that had swiftly become the basis of the Portuguese economy. In three papal bulls, Nicholas V and Calixtus III extolled the accomplishments of Prince Henry and affirmed that Portugal had carried out the good work of the Church in conquering Moorish lands in Morocco and enslaving Moslems and Africans. Further, Portugal's slave trade was praised for bringing converts into the Church; the seizure of pagan lands was authorized; and other nations were forbidden

Above, a portrait of Henry the Navigator, the architect of Portugal's early program of exploration. Left, a carrack, or cargo vessel, used for trade with India.

from encroaching on lands already discovered by the Portuguese.

These papal pronouncements set the capstone on Henry the Navigator's long and productive career. When he died in 1460, some 1,500 miles of African coastline had been discovered and partially mapped; the Azores and Madeira were active colonies; and the long-standing barrier presented by Cape Bojador had been overcome.

Portuguese captains made noteworthy progress in the two decades following Henry's death, venturing down the northwestern coast of Africa past present-day Sierra Leone and Liberia into the Gulf of Guinea. Events moved rapidly after the accession in 1481 of John II, who stands alongside Prince Henry as one of the founders of Portugal's empire. The new king ordered the construction of a castle on the African coast at Mina, on the Gulf of Guinea, to defend the trade route and serve as a trading post—a bold move since the climate of the area was notoriously inimical to Europeans. A Portuguese official who served at Mina saw divine retribution as the reason why so many of his comrades were lost to tropical diseases: "It seems that for our sins, or for some inscrutable judgment of God . . . He has placed a striking angel with a flaming sword of deadly fevers."

The boldness John displayed in placing a colony in equatorial Africa was just one of the qualities that led Portuguese historians to call him the Perfect Prince— the embodiment of Machiavelli's calculating model ruler described in the author's famous work, *The Prince*. In the Machiavellian mode John made imaginative use of rumor—an effective tool for dealing with credulous seamen. John instructed the commander of the Mina expedition, for example, to destroy two heavy cargo ships at Mina, then later spread the story that they had been lost on the trip home. Consequently, other European nations, possessing only similar, clumsy ships, were hampered in their attempts to capitalize on Portugal's African trade route by sailors fearful of shipping out on any vessel other than a Portuguese caravel. This rumor was taken seriously even at the Portuguese court, where one of John's most experienced navigators repeatedly asserted that he could take a heavy ship to Mina and bring it back safely. With feigned impatience John publicly called the man a fool, then privately apologized and revealed his ruse.

During the time of Mina's settlement, the Portuguese were enjoying a tremendous advantage over other European nations in both ship design and navigation. Inspired by Prince Henry's school at Sagres, John established a court committee of mathemati-

The sixteenth-century Tower of Belém (left) was built to protect the narrow channel of the Tagus River that flows through Lisbon to the Atlantic. Right, King Alfonso V. Above, Alfonso's wife, Isabel, and above right, their son John II, called the Perfect Prince.

cians called the Junta, which was given the task of solving a new and vexing navigational problem. Portuguese navigators had been able to determine their latitude by sighting the North Star through an astrolabe and measuring the apparent distance of the star from the horizon; John's sea captains, however, were now regularly exploring waters south of the equator where the North Star was not visible. Eventually mariners learned to navigate by the Southern Cross, but before that constellation had been identified John's Junta came up with an interim solution: It drew up mathematical tables giving the declination, or celestial position, of the sun at various lati-

tudes and times. By consulting these tables at sea, a navigator could now determine his position by measuring the height of the sun with his quadrant.

The improvements in navigational instruments and methods led to refinements in the field of cartography. Portuguese maps of the fifteenth and sixteenth centuries were the best in Europe, and foreign spies in Lisbon often attempted to buy or steal them. By early in the sixteenth century, the Portuguese had resorted to safeguarding their maps by giving them the status of state secrets—royal decree forbade the circulation of maps showing the sailing routes south of the Congo River in Africa. And yet, as useful and

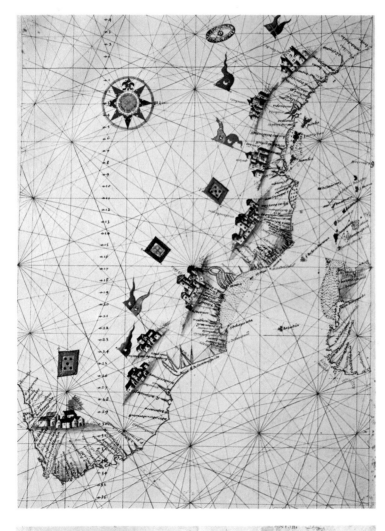

Preceding pages, an aerial view of the Cape of Good Hope, discovered by Bartholomeu Dias in 1488. Left, a sixteenth-century map depicting the coast of eastern Africa and the cities discovered there by the Portuguese.

Left, two African tribesmen portrayed hunting. Soon after Portuguese explorers arrived on Africa's shores, slave traders established bases there. They sold their human cargoes first in Europe and then in Brazil, where the growth of sugar plantations had created a lucrative slave market. Above, a pillory used to confine slaves at the Brazilian colony of Bahia.

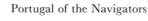

accurate as these maps were, no Portuguese pilot trusted them completely. Many captains followed what they called "Nature's signs"—the color of the sea, currents, types of seaweed, fish and birds, and the prevailing winds—to provide an approximate idea of their location. Even in the early seventeenth century a Portuguese mariner wrote that many shoals and islands were not marked on maps and that a good captain relied less on his charts than on "God and a good lookout."

During the 1480s, John's explorers continued to progress down the African coast. On two voyages Diogo Cam discovered the mouth of the Congo River and sailed as far south as Cape Cross in southwestern Africa, but he failed to find the end of the continent and the route to the Indies that remained the elusive goal of the Crown. Yet any pessimism at the Lisbon court was instantly dispelled by the return from Africa of Captain João Afonso de Aveiro, who brought with him an envoy from the northwestern coastal kingdom of Benin. The envoy reported that at a twenty-moon (or month) march east of the Benin coast there lived a monarch named Ogane who distributed Christian crosses to his subjects as a sign of his beneficence. Curiously, he always remained concealed behind a curtain, allowing only a foot to be

John II (right) ascended the Portuguese throne in 1481 and rapidly revived the program of exploration that had stagnated for two decades. He sponsored astronomical and mathematical research on the problems of navigation and dispatched illustrious captains like Diogo Cam and Bartholomeu Dias down the African coast. John believed, correctly, that the route to the Indies could be discovered by sailing south, and rejected Christopher Columbus' plan to reach Asia by sailing west. Below, the castle of São Jorge in Lisbon, originally built in the fifth century A.D. and expanded in the ninth century.

The court of the Fortunate King

Precious cargoes from Asia and Africa, brought up the Tagus River for the first time in the late fifteenth century, transformed the royal court of Manuel I, in Lisbon, into one of the most colorful in Europe. The wealthy king delighted in exotic pleasures. He was the first Christian king to own an elephant and a rhinoceros, choosing to display them by staging a battle between the two. (The elephant simply ran off.) The king also was fond of parading in the company of an Iranian retainer, who rode with a leopard perched on his horse. Other more conventional pastimes that attracted Manuel's interest were horse racing, partying, and picnicking to the ever-present accompaniment of musicians.

Left, a miniature (ca. 1600) from a codex depicting a royal audience, possibly with John II or Manuel I. Under Manuel I, Lisbon became a showcase of European culture.

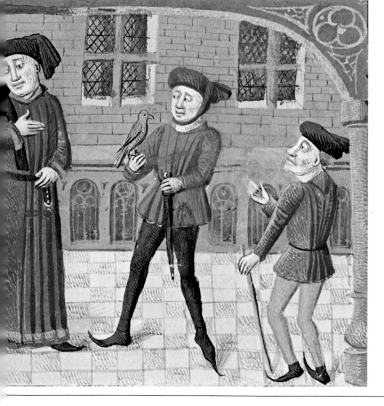

Monasteries, endowed by the king, provided most of the education in medieval Portugal. Below, a monk, acting as a scribe of the court. Above, two gentlemen in the rich robes worn at court.

Above, a nobleman and his lady on a fifteenth-century picnic. Picnicking was one of the favorite pastimes of Manuel and the Portuguese courtiers.

Below, a group of courtiers. The bird held by the second man from the right may be a parrot, in vogue at court and imported at great expense from Africa.

Manuel I (left) has been called the Fortunate King because his reign, from 1495 to 1521, saw the creation of the Asian empire for which his predecessors had long labored. At home, Manuel promoted architecture, the arts, and education, and took stern measures to protect Jews—though only temporarily—from persecution. Below, an official document of 1515 bearing Manuel's name and the nation's coat of arms.

seen. The fantastical elements in this account led John's scholars to conclude that Ogane was the long-sought Prester John and calculated that the twenty-moon march from the western coast placed his kingdom in Abyssinia (present-day Ethiopia).

The hope of finding Prester John had never been relinquished by the Portuguese, so it was amidst great excitement that John ordered the navigator Bartholomeu Dias to fit out a fleet of caravels for a journey around Africa to Abyssinia. At the same time, the king dispatched two agents, Afonso de Paiva and Pedro de Covilhão, to travel to the Near East and gather information there about both Prester John and the spice trade.

Dias sailed from Lisbon in the summer of 1487 with two caravels and a supply ship. No contemporary account of his voyage has survived, but it is known that Dias had followed the African coast, in the face of strong head winds, to a point about six hundred miles north of the end of the continent, when the wind shifted and blew him directly south—

out of the sight of land and into bitterly cold weather. When Dias finally turned east he was unable to locate land, so he set his course for the north and struck the African coast at Mossel Bay, about two hundred miles northeast of the southern tip of the continent. Africa had been rounded at last.

Dias sailed on for a few days until the entreaties of his crew, fearful of running out of food and exhausted by the freezing, stormy weather, forced him to turn back. On the return voyage he passed a promontory that he named the Cape of Storms, after the rough seas that tossed his caravels; upon his arrival at Lisbon in December of 1488, King John, in a burst of optimism, rechristened it the Cape of Good Hope.

Although John's two agents, Paiva and Covilhão, had set out on their journey a few months before Dias' departure, nothing had been heard from them. By way of the Aegean island of Rhodes and the Mediterranean port of Alexandria the pair had traveled to Aden, on the southern shore of Arabia, where they separated: Paiva continued south to Abyssinia and

Left, Leonora of Austria, who became the third wife of Manuel I. In 1530, nine years after Manuel's death, she married another king, Francis I of France. The marriage was to reconcile Francis and Charles V of Spain, mortal enemies for twenty-seven years.

Lisbon's harbor (above) was one of the busiest in Europe during Manuel's reign, rivaling Venice as the continent's chief marketplace of Asian goods. Spices such as pepper, ginger, cinnamon, and saffron were prized commodities in the India-Europe trade.

Covilhão turned east to India. Covilhão surveyed the Moslem trading centers at Goa and Calicut on the western coast of India and at Hormuz in the Persian Gulf off Iran; from there he sailed to the gold-trading city of Sofala on the southeastern coast of Africa. By the end of 1490, Covilhão had traveled to Cairo to meet Paiva, but the agent never reappeared. As Covilhão was preparing to return to Lisbon, he was found by two Portuguese Jews who presented him with orders from King John to continue the search for Prester John.

Following the king's commands, Covilhão made his way from Cairo to Abyssinia where he met the

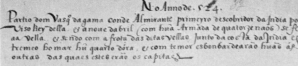

Founding father of the empire

The choice of Vasco da Gama to lead the first Portuguese expedition around Africa to India was a fortunate one. The skilled navigator possessed the courage, tenacity, and ruthlessness needed to lead recalcitrant crews into unknown waters and to plant the roots of Portugal's empire in hostile lands. On the voyage of 1497–1498 da Gama was forced to quell a mutiny in the midst of violent weather as he warily sailed up the coast of eastern Africa, where Moslems twice laid ambushes for the fleet. In 1498, da Gama bravely strode past threatening mobs in India to secure the cooperation of the local ruler. On his second voyage to India (1502) he was less the ambassador of good will and more the gunboat diplomat, setting fire to a ship full of civilians and bombarding the city of Calicut. After spending several years in retirement in Portugal, da Gama returned to India as viceroy in 1524, and died shortly thereafter.

With a fleet of fifteen ships (above left) da Gama embarked on his second voyage to India to secure alliances with friendly rulers and overpower those who resisted. This expedition culminated in an attack on the city of Calicut.

After da Gama's expeditions, the Cape of Good Hope (above), once an unreachable destination, became just another landmark on the long voyage around Africa. Below, an ancient map of Indian waters.

Vasco da Gama (above) was governor of the fishing port of Sines when John II selected him to lead an expedition to explore India.

Below, a document, bearing da Gama's signature, concerning Portugal's trade monopoly on the Indian subcontinent.

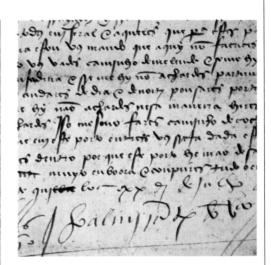

A sixteenth-century Flemish tapestry (left) depicts da Gama's arrival in Calicut in 1498. Da Gama is shown handing a message to the lord of the city. Calicut's inhabitants actually gave da Gama's fleet a hostile reception, prompting an early Portuguese departure as well as brutal reprisals during da Gama's second expedition to India.

In 1493, Pope Alexander VI (right) attempted to guarantee Spain's dominion over the lands of the New World by issuing a bull that divided the world into Portuguese and Spanish territory. Portugal's protests forced a settlement of the issue. Known as an astute politician and administrator, Alexander also earned the title the Wayward Pope because of his notorious involvements with his many mistresses. He fathered several children, the most famous of whom were Cesare and Lucrezia Borgia.

Immediately below, two ships of the Portuguese fleet—commanded by Pedro Álvares Cabral—that landed in Brazil in 1500. Bottom left, an early sixteenth-century map of the known world. Bottom right, a 1561 map of South America, revealing the rapid advances in exploration.

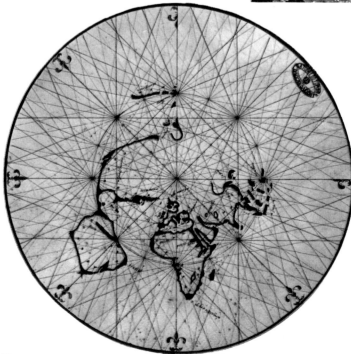

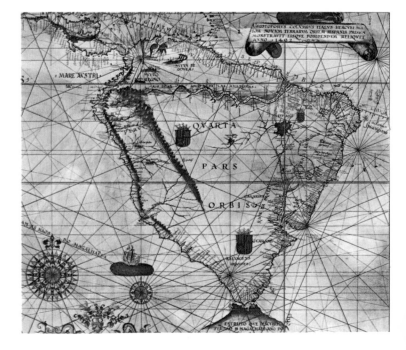

Above, the papal bull issued by Alexander VI in 1493, called Inter caetera, *which favored Spain's designs on the New World. The Treaty of Tordesillas (right), negotiated by Spain and Portugal the following year, superseded the bull.*

Christian monarch who may very well have been the inspiration for the Prester John legend in its fifteenth-century version. Covilhão discovered, predictably, that the accounts of the monarch's wealth and military power had been greatly exaggerated. Although Abyssinia traded in gold and ivory, it was not a rich kingdom. In fact, its army was too weak to defend the nation's own borders, let alone fight a world war against Islam. Once in Abyssinia, Covilhão was not permitted to leave—although the king presented him with a wife and land, hoping to ease his homesickness. Other Portuguese travelers found Covilhão there around 1520 and pressed the king to release him, to no avail. He died in Abyssinia sometime after 1526.

When Dias returned to Lisbon in 1488, he told King John's court of his discovery of the cape marking the southern extent of Africa. Among those present was a Genoese navigator—Christopher Columbus. Columbus was undoubtedly disheartened to hear of Dias' accomplishment because he had come to King John to present his own proposal for reaching the Indies by sailing west to Cipango—Japan—which Marco Polo had described around 1300 in the account of his seventeen-year stay in the empire of Kublai Khan. Columbus had first advanced his ideas

to the Portuguese court in 1485, but John had rejected Columbus' proposal after the Junta found fundamental errors in Columbus' calculation of the size of the globe. The voyage of Dias convinced John that he had no need of Columbus and his wild schemes, so the Genoese navigator took his plan to Spain, to the rival court of Castile, where King Ferdinand and Queen Isabella were persuaded in 1492 to give their support.

Columbus' first voyage brought him to San Salvador Island, in the Bahamas, part of several island groups later referred to as the West Indies, which he took to be on the outer reaches of Asia. On his return to Europe, Columbus rushed to Lisbon, where, after being ushered into the court, he told a fantastically embellished story of the gold-roofed houses and jewels he had found—which would have been put in the hands of Portugal if only John had believed him.

John believed little of what Columbus claimed beyond the fact that new islands had been discovered. He also pointed out to the admiral that his discoveries were apparently south of the latitude of the Canaries, thus within the Portuguese sphere of dominion as set down by the 1479 Treaty of Alcaçovas. John then stated his intentions of dispatching a Portuguese fleet to claim these new lands—a plan that was to temper the joy of the Castilian court over its new possessions.

The Portuguese navigator Ferdinand Magellan (above) presented his plan for a voyage around the world to the Spanish court after having been rejected by his own king, Manuel I.

The first voyage around the world

Roughly a quarter century after Columbus sailed west from Europe with the hope of finding Asia, the Portuguese navigator Ferdinand Magellan set out to complete that mission. In September of 1519, Magellan, in service to Spain, sailed for South America with a fleet of five ships. In October of 1520 he discovered and sailed through the strait that now bears his name. The following month Magellan began his journey across the ocean he called Pacific (after its calm seas). By the end of the four-month crossing, his crew members were reduced to eating rats as well as the leather rigging on the sails before the fleet reached Guam. In August of 1521 Magellan landed on one of the Philippine Islands, where he was killed in a skirmish with the natives. After another thirteen months a lone ship reached Spanish shores with only eighteen surviving crewmen.

*The **Victoria** (below) was the only ship from Magellan's fleet of five to complete the circumnavigation.*

Above and below left, two views of the Strait of Magellan, which separates the Tierra del Fuego archipelago from the South American continent and links the Atlantic and Pacific. The strait provides a route between the oceans that is safer than the stormy passage around Cape Horn.

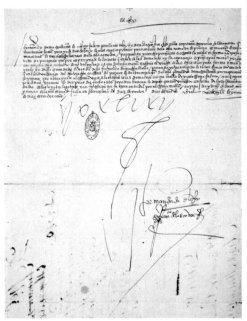

Left, Battista Agnese's world map of the 1540s showing the route of Magellan's fleet. The map reveals Europe's limited knowledge of the world: The extent of eastern Asia is unknown, and the interior regions of both Asia and America have been left blank. Right, Emperor Charles V's orders to the Spanish officers of the exploring fleet to submit to Magellan's commands. This imperial edict did not prevent a mutiny off South America that nearly decimated the fleet.

Left, an illustration from the diary of Antonio Pigafetta, one of the few members of the expedition to survive the entire voyage. The drawing depicts Guam, which Pigafetta termed the Island of Thieves after the theft of a boat by natives who tried to abscond with some of the fleet's provisions. Pigafetta wrote an account of the voyage which was translated into several languages and made him a sought-after storyteller in European courts.

The greatest architectural achievement of Manuel I's reign is the monastery at Belém (below), built in the sumptuous Manueline style that combines Moorish, Asian, and European influences. Above, an illustration from Manuel's letter to the pope recounting the takeover of Portugal from the Moors. Facing page, the funeral of Manuel in 1521.

King Ferdinand hastily secured a papal bull that placed the disputed territories under the Spanish flag, but after John's vehement protests he agreed to negotiate the matter with Lisbon. In 1494 the two countries settled on the Treaty of Tordesillas, by which the world was divided into Spanish and Portuguese hemispheres along a north-south line 370 leagues west of the Canaries. An earlier draft had set the line at 270 leagues from the islands but John's negotiators insisted on the more distant line. Portugal's intransigence on this point has led scholars to speculate that the Portuguese must have had some knowledge of the geography of the South American continent—perhaps as a result of a voyage of exploration prior to Columbus'—because the new line put Brazil into their possession.

The Portuguese were well aware that the lands discovered by Columbus were not the (East) Indies and continued their plan to reach Asia by way of the African sea route. Nine years elapsed, however, between Dias' return in 1488 and the departure of the next major exploring voyage—a delay that has never been completely explained. According to some scholars the reason may be attributed to King John's profound depression after the death of his son and heir in a riding accident, a depression from which he never recovered and which led to his own death in 1495. But other historians have suggested that the Portuguese were dissatisfied with the route they had always followed along the coast of Africa because of strong winds. It is conjectured that John and his successor, Manuel I, ordered a series of secret voyages in the

Left, a bronze statue, roughly sixteen inches high, of a Portuguese soldier made by a Beninese sculptor. The style of the soldier's armor dates the work to the sixteenth century, when Portugal carried on a brief trade with the African coastal kingdom of Benin. The statue was made for the palace of the Beninese king to indicate that he had accepted the presence of the Portuguese explorers and traders in his kingdom.

Below, a decorative bronze plaque showing a man playing slit drums. The rosettes in the background are similar to motifs of Nubian art, from the Nile Valley region of Southern Egypt and northern Sudan, and indicate that the Beninese may have traded with the Egyptians. Like the other bronzes on these pages, this plaque is now housed in the British Museum.

The bronze sculptures of Benin

When Portuguese explorers first reached the African kingdom of Benin (in present-day Nigeria) in the 1480s they were amazed at the high level of civilization they encountered. The nation boasted a large, well-maintained capital city, with a royal palace adorned by striking bronze statues and plaques. Benin's artisans made their bronzes by a process now called *cire perdue*—French for "lost wax"—in which a plaster or clay mold was coated with wax and then coated again with plaster or clay. The whole was heated until the wax melted, leaving a gap that was filled with molten bronze. When the bronze had cooled, the molds were broken off, creating a hollow sculpture that could be filed to add details. Many Beninese lost-wax bronzes are depictions of kings and queens that may have been used in religious rites; others are purely decorative.

Right, a bust of a Beninese princess. She wears a cone-shaped headdress and neck rings, probably of gold.

João de Castro

One of the heroes of Portuguese history celebrated in Luis Vaz de Camoëns' epic, *The Lusiads,* is João de Castro, who made his mark as a navigator, cartographer, and governor of India. Castro was born in 1500 to a noble family and was educated at court where he studied under the famous geographer and mathematician Pedro Nunes. After serving as a staff officer on a military expedition to Morocco in 1518, Castro settled down to a quiet life in Portugal, studying botany and navigational theory, until John III asked him to command a ship sailing to India in 1538. On the long voyage Castro experimented with the ship's compass and was the first to observe that the needle was influenced by iron on board. This connection explained variations in compass readings that had puzzled previous captains. Castro also tested a new navigational instrument invented by Nunes, and made cartographic calculations for his former tutor that indirectly led to the development of Mercator projection—one of the greatest breakthroughs in the history of map making.

Once in India, Castro made detailed observations of the African and Asian coastlines, which he published in three *roteiros,* or navigational guides, and attempted to answer the age-old question of why the Red Sea was red. In 1542 Castro returned to Portugal and was almost immediately dispatched to India again by the king, this time as governor. In 1548, just a few days after the king promoted him to viceroy, Castro died of wounds received in a battle with the Moslems.

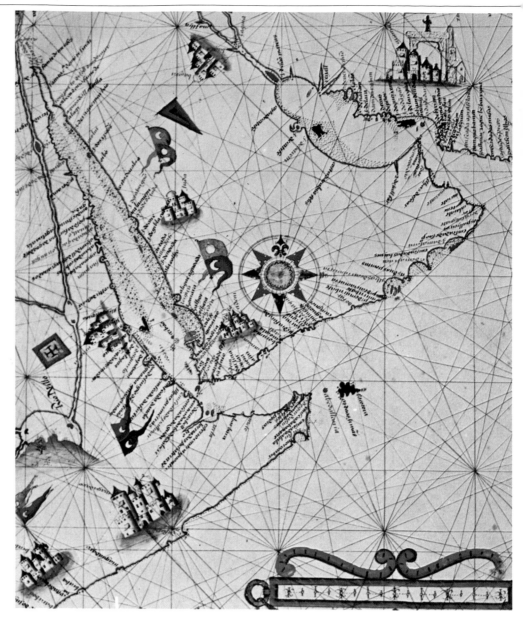

Late in 1540, João de Castro undertook a perilous six-month voyage in the Red Sea, which was controlled by the Egyptians. Castro published the results of this and other voyages in a map (above) of the Red Sea, the Arabian Peninsula, and the Persian Gulf. Castro's interest in navigation led to advances in cartography.

Below left, a port on the Persian coast. Immediately below, an Arabian port shown on a sixteenth-century map. Castro's explorations took him along the entire coast of the Arabian Peninsula and throughout the Persian Gulf at a time when sea battles between Portuguese and Moslem ships were still common.

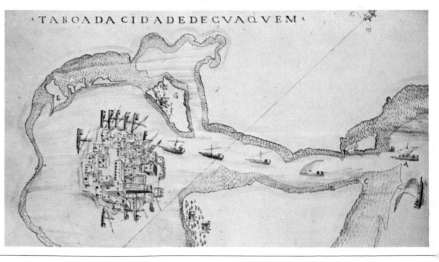

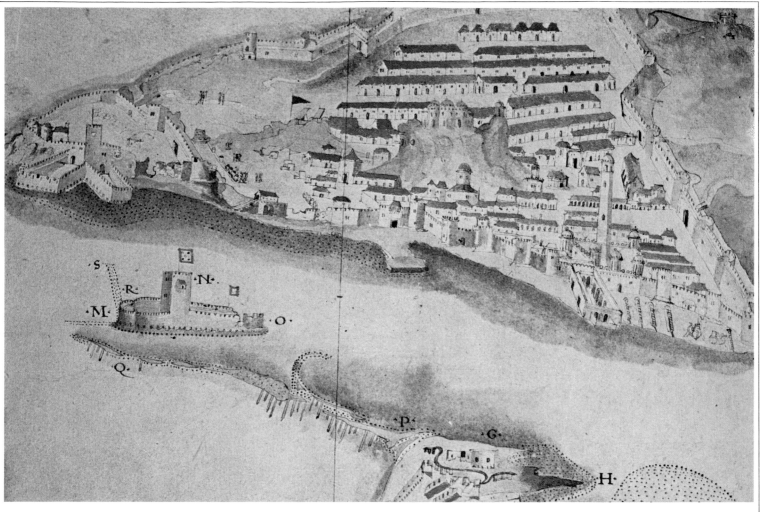

Castro illustrated his roteiros with detailed drawings of cities, topographical features, and vignettes. Top, his sketch of the city of Diu in India. Arabs on land (immediately above) attack a Portuguese fleet at the Red Sea port now known as Port Sudan. Above right, Portuguese ships on the Red Sea. Right, ships on the bay at Mesewa in Ethiopia.

open waters of the Atlantic to find more favorable prevailing winds.

King John and his geographers were aware that the Indies lay east of Africa, but that was virtually all they knew. No one had any notion of how long a voyage to the Indies would be, which route should be taken after the limit of the known world had been passed at the Cape of Good Hope, or what perils on sea and on land the voyagers would have to face. The success of the attempt would rest on the degree of the captain's resourcefulness, courage, determination, diplomacy, and nautical skill. These qualifications were well met by a nobleman named Vasco da Gama.

Little is known of da Gama's early life. His sea experience was not recorded; even his birthdate is a matter of conjecture. Surviving descriptions suggest that he was a brave man with a quick temper. Kings John and Manuel (the latter confirming John's choice of da Gama to lead the voyage) were aware of the captain's darker side, and yet selected him precisely because of it. Portuguese seamen often grew recalcitrant in the face of danger and needed to be bullied into obedience. In addition, the entrenched powers of Asia were known for their especially fierce resistance to the European interlopers, requiring equally fierce opposition.

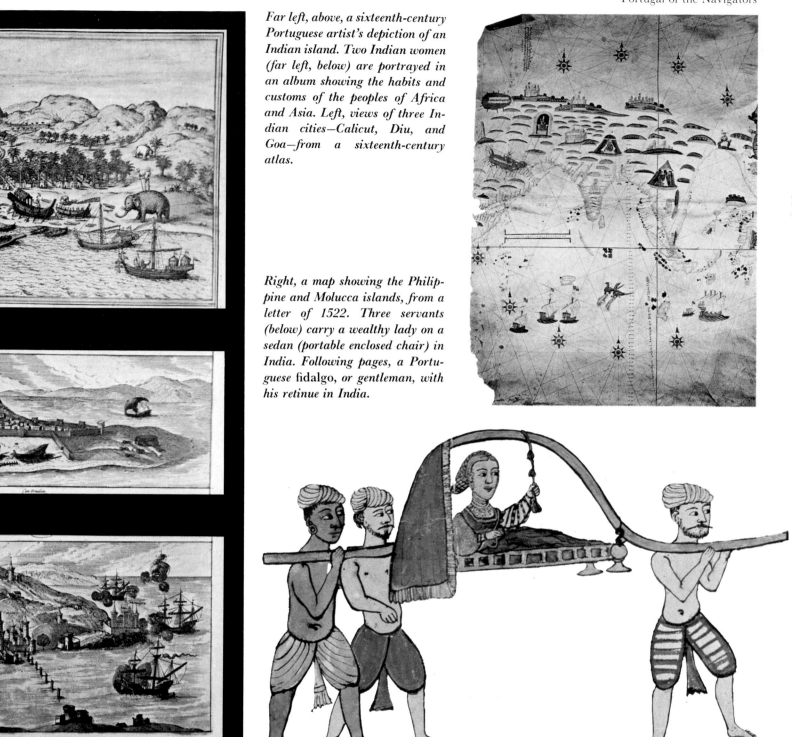

Far left, above, a sixteenth-century Portuguese artist's depiction of an Indian island. Two Indian women (far left, below) are portrayed in an album showing the habits and customs of the peoples of Africa and Asia. Left, views of three Indian cities—Calicut, Diu, and Goa—from a sixteenth-century atlas.

Right, a map showing the Philippine and Molucca islands, from a letter of 1522. Three servants (below) carry a wealthy lady on a sedan (portable enclosed chair) in India. Following pages, a Portuguese fidalgo, or gentleman, with his retinue in India.

After an emotional prayer service on the banks of the Tagus River, da Gama's fleet of four vessels set sail in July of 1497. The course it followed supports the theory that the Portuguese had scouted a route different from the one Dias had taken nine years earlier. Da Gama allowed the winds to carry him in a southwesterly direction across the Atlantic (how far west is debated) until he caught the prevailing wind from the north that drove him swiftly south. When da Gama's fleet turned east and finally made landfall at St. Helena Bay, it had been out of sight of land for ninety-six days—the longest such voyage ever made to that time. It was a marvel of navigation, for da Gama

had struck the continent only a hundred miles north of his intended goal, the Cape of Good Hope.

Da Gama took his bearings, and after an unfriendly brush with the natives he sailed around the Cape, where the fleet was struck by a storm. Even though Dias and da Gama had designed a heavier ship for the inhospitable south African seas, the vessels began to take in water at an alarming rate. With difficulty the captains quieted their crews, and after the storm abated, they landed the fleet and bought food from the natives. When they again set sail yet another storm developed—so violent that the crews verged on mutiny. According to one account, da

Rule and misrule in the empire

Portugal's Asian empire, officially called Estado da India—the State of India—eventually extended from Sofala in Africa to Macao in China. Francisco de Almeida, the first viceroy of the Indian empire, and his successor, Afonso de Albuquerque, who ruled with the lesser title and power of governor, established a string of forts and trading stations in Asia, as well as a system of naval patrols to protect them. Because the officials were paid only pittances, they resorted to trading on the side, which quickly led to corruption. Governor Nunho da Cunha was accused of extortion and recalled, but the prospect of similar humiliation did not deter his successors. In 1720, John V attempted to curtail questionable trading practices and increased salaries in compensation. Nonetheless, trafficking in favors, buying and selling offices, and private trading with royal funds continued because officials—mostly of the nobility—felt it was their right to enrich themselves. In the words of one governor, the malefactors had "elastic consciences . . . and [they] think they are going on a pilgrimage to Jerusalem when they steal."

Francisco de Almeida

Afonso de Albuquerque

Garcia de Noronha

Duarte de Menezes

Nunho da Cunha

Martim Afonso de Sousa

Left, Portuguese cargo ships of the type used in the India trade. Below, a fifteenth-century map of Ceylon, which was called the Supremely Beautiful Island. The Portuguese first landed on Ceylon in 1505 and, taking advantage of a civil war among the island's three principal rulers, quickly conquered the coastal regions. Ceylon became one of Portugal's most important Asian colonies; it produced cinnamon of the best quality, which commanded three times the standard price. Despite its importance, Ceylon was governed by incompetent officials who lost much of their territory to the Dutch in the 1630s and were completely expelled two decades later.

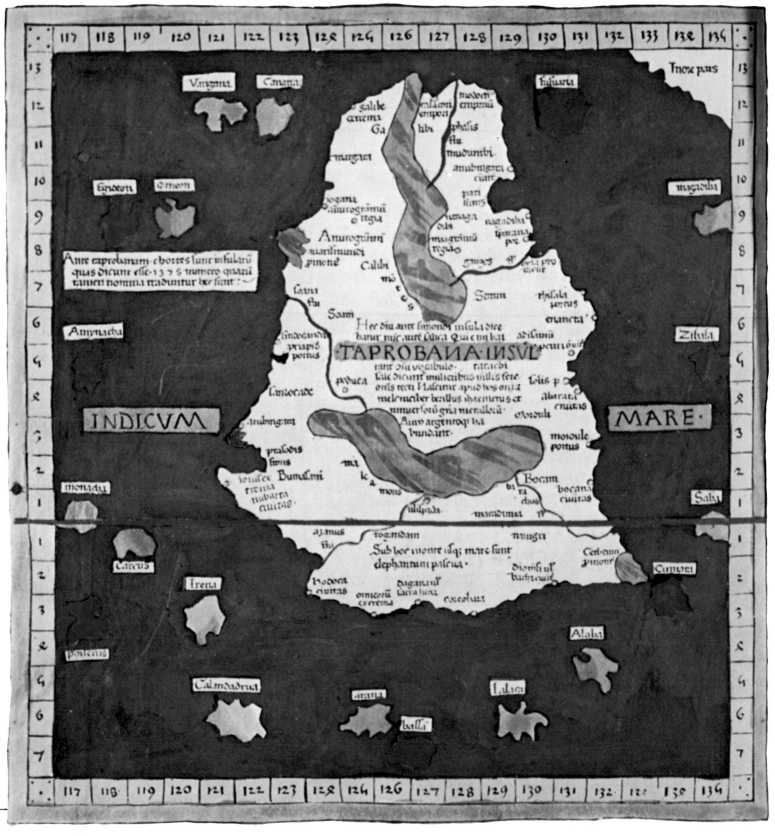

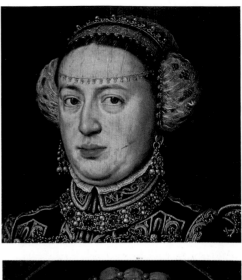

The Portuguese established amiable relations with the emperor of Abyssinia—the Negus—early in the sixteenth century and built a fort at Gondar (above). In 1535, when Abyssinia was invaded by Somali tribesmen, the Negus sent an appeal for help to John III (the text of his letter is at right), who dispatched an army to Abyssinia two years later.

The lure of Prester John

During the twelfth century rumors spread throughout Europe about a rich Christian kingdom in Asia ruled by a powerful monarch called Prester John. The stories were supported by letters from this king—later proved to be forgeries—and by garbled accounts of wars in remote Asia. No one believed these tales more eagerly than the Portuguese, who actually succeeded, late in the fifteenth century, in finding the kingdom that may have inspired the Prester John legend. A report from Africa led John II to dispatch an agent to Abyssinia, a country on an isolated plateau, in the area now known as Ethiopia. There the traveler found an emperor who was indeed a Christian, though of the heretical Coptic sect. Most disappointing, his realm was neither wealthy nor powerful. The legend that had for centuries intrigued Europe soon dropped out of circulation.

Facing page, top left, King John III, who ruled from 1521 to 1557. Portugal's empire reached its greatest heights during his reign. John acquired several Asian possessions by conquest and ousted the French from Brazil. Agriculture and the economy in Portugal itself, however, declined. John's wife, Catherine (near left), served as regent during the youth of King Sebastian. John's grandniece Maria (below left) married Alessandro Farnese, a diplomat and general who served Spain.

Gama was compelled to throw his navigational instruments overboard to convince the sailors he would never turn back.

In early March of 1498, da Gama dropped anchor off an African city, and a small flotilla of boats came out to greet the visitors. Through a seaman who spoke Arabic, da Gama learned that the town was called Mozambique, that it was controlled by Moslem merchants who carried on a brisk trade with India, and that he had passed a far richer city—Sofala—to the south. The ruler of the city, under the impression that the strangers were Moslems like himself, came out to greet da Gama, who entertained the potentate with a display of gunfire and secured pilots to guide the fleet farther north. By an unfortunate stroke of luck three Abyssinian Christians came aboard the flagship and fell on their knees before an image of Saint Gabriel, thus revealing to the Moslems that the Portuguese visitors were Christians. That night several armed boats attacked the fleet, but it was able to slip away with one of the native pilots. The pilot directed da Gama to a place a few miles north of Mozambique where he could obtain fresh water; when a party went ashore, however, it was ambushed, escaping only under cover of gunfire from the fleet. Although da Gama ordered the pilot tied to the mast and whipped, the punishment proved to have little effect, for he subsequently led da Gama into another trap at the city of Mombasa, where the fleet narrowly escaped destruction.

Da Gama got a much more hospitable reception at the city of Malindi, which was a traditional enemy of Mombasa. The ruler of Malindi supplied the fleet with new water casks and provided da Gama with one of the most eminent pilots in Africa, who guided the fleet safely to the city of Calicut, on the western coast of India, on May 14, 1498.

Da Gama's voyage was one of the greatest achievements of Renaissance exploration, rivaled only by the 1519–1521 voyage of Magellan, a Portuguese captain in service to Spain who crossed the Atlantic and Pacific to reach the Philippines. Some fifty years later,

Above, a portrait of Luis Vaz de Camoëns, Portugal's most eminent poet. As a youth Camoëns was sent to Africa—after his love affair with a lady at court was discovered—where he lost an eye in battle. While in India he wrote his famous epic, The Lusiads.

Luis Vaz de Camoëns

"My theme is the daring and renown of the Portuguese," wrote Luis Vaz de Camoëns in his work *The Lusiads,* the national epic of Portugal. Camoëns won little renown for himself during his lifetime, but is now regarded as Portugal's greatest poet. The details surrounding his life are vague. He was born around 1524, may have received a university education, and enlisted in the army in 1533, serving seventeen years in India. While there, Camoëns wrote *The Lusiads,* a poem in ten cantos that is structured around the story of Vasco da Gama (a distant relative of the author) and his voyage to the East. In the tradition of Virgil's *Aeneid,* Camoëns' hero, da Gama, relates episodes from the history of Portugal, at home and abroad. Especially poignant is the tragic love story of Inés de Castro, a Castilian noblewoman who was brutally slain for her illicit affair with a Portuguese prince. In addition to Portuguese history, Camoëns' poem weaves Portuguese mythology into the context of da Gama's journeys, including descriptions of the fabulous Island of Love, where Portuguese sailors dally with sea nymphs.

Camoëns returned to his homeland in 1570 and published his poem two years later. Although it attracted the attention of the king, who then provided the poet with a small pension, Camoëns died in obscurity in 1580.

da Gama's feat, and the captain himself, were immortalized by Luis Vaz de Camoëns in his poem *The Lusiads*—the national epic of Portugal.

The arrival of the Portuguese in India was a breakthrough in world history on a par with Columbus' discovery of America. It joined the Old World to the even older civilizations of Asia, hitherto isolated by the Islamic powers of the Middle East. A new period of Asian history had begun, a period which a modern Indian historian has, somewhat sardonically, christened the Vasco da Gama epoch, dating from 1498 to 1945—the four and a half centuries of European domination of Asia.

The era began unimpressively when the captain called on the ruler of Calicut—the Samuri, or Lord of the Sea. Da Gama attempted to awe the Asian by expounding on the wealth and puissance of the Portuguese king, but King Manuel's gifts—a few hats, some cloth, bits of coral, and other baubles—failed to impress the Samuri. In fact, he was so taken aback by this measly offering from a supposedly rich monarch that he declined to enter into any agreements with da Gama. The Samuri was also under pressure from the Moslem merchants to avoid dealing with the foreigners, and the Moslems were prepared to pay handsome bribes to back their requests. The Moslem merchants

The east coast of Africa boasted several flourishing cities at the time the Portuguese first arrived. Below, from left, Kilwa, Sofala, and Mombasa. Above, a view of the Portuguese fort at Mombasa.

refused to buy the cargoes of oil, honey, and other Portuguese goods that da Gama offered for sale, and jostled and threatened the Portuguese seamen when they came ashore.

In spite of the difficulties facing the Portuguese, da Gama managed to fill his holds with spices and set sail. After a difficult return voyage, during which da Gama's brother Paul and a great many seamen died from scurvy, da Gama triumphantly sailed up the Tagus in September 1499 to be richly rewarded by the king. King Manuel proclaimed da Gama's discoveries throughout Europe and immediately took for himself the grand title of Lord of the Conquest, Nav-

igation, and Commerce of Ethiopia, Arabia, Persia, and India.

King Manuel acted quickly to take control of the Indian trade route that da Gama had discovered. Just six months after da Gama's return, Pedro Álvares Cabral set out from Lisbon with a fleet of thirteen ships piloted by the best navigators in Portugal, including Bartholomeu Dias, and provisioned for a year and a half. Cabral followed a route similar to the one da Gama had pioneered, sailing southwest across the Atlantic, and touched land at Brazil on April 22, 1500. Historians are still debating, however, whether Cabral truly discovered Brazil or whether Portugal

Caravels (left), whose sails were decorated with red crosses, were the workhorses of the Portuguese exploring fleet. Above, the ruins of the fortified palace built by the Portuguese at Kilwa.

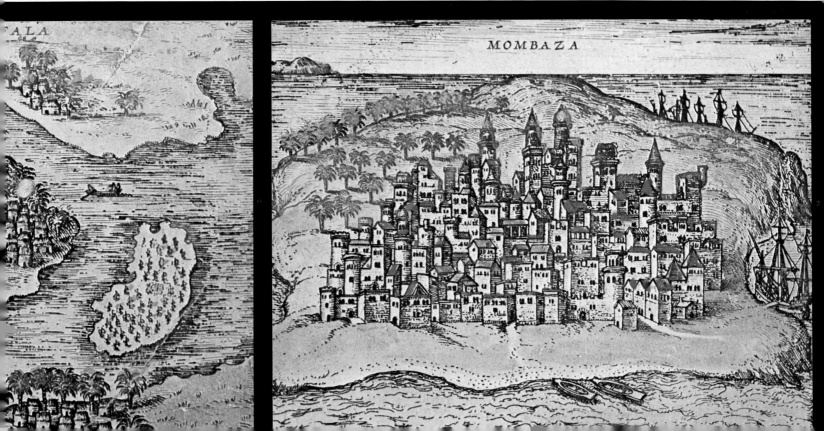

had already known of its existence and Cabral had merely conducted an official mission of "discovery" to assert a proper claim.

Cabral spent a few days on the South American shore, ordered one ship to return to Lisbon with a report of the new lands, and set sail for Africa. The fleet soon encountered violent storms that sank three of the ships, among them Dias'. After surviving another storm lasting twenty days, the battered fleet rounded the Cape of Good Hope and headed directly for the friendly port of Malindi. Once again a pilot was provided to guide the Portuguese to India, where the Moslems were beginning to organize resistance to the Portuguese usurpers. At Calicut the Moslems killed a Portuguese trader, and Cabral decided on a bloody retaliation: He burned ten Moslem ships, killed the crews, and fired on the city. The show of force made for a quiet reception at the cities of Cochin and Cannanore, where the fleet took on cargo and headed home. The voyage was a rough one. Only six ships of the original thirteen returned to Lisbon, but the rich cargo of spices they carried more than paid for the lost vessels.

Though some Portuguese officials expressed dismay at the violent turn of events in the Indies and argued for a peaceful policy, the king and his captains were intent on pressing their naval superiority over the Moslems to gain the upper hand as rapidly as possible. The Portuguese advantage lay in the design of the ships—larger and sturdier than the Moslem vessels, which were not really equipped for warfare. In addition, the Portuguese were resolute in their war policy whereas the Moslem and Hindu powers of Asia offered only passive resistance. The rulers of the Asian interior gave little thought to the war at sea and on the coast, considering it a matter for the merchants to handle themselves. Nonetheless the struggle was a bitter one, lasting over a decade.

In 1502, da Gama left Lisbon on his second voyage to the Indies with fifteen ships, followed by another fleet of six ships. Though the main purpose of da Gama's voyage was trade, part of the combined fleet was earmarked for a permanent squadron to patrol Indian waters, establish Portuguese supremacy on the seas, and enforce the new policy requiring Moslem ships to buy a *cartaz,* or license, from the Crown to carry cargo. Da Gama, resolved to make a show of force at the first opportunity, displayed a ruthless brutality that previous Portuguese captains had not demonstrated. While sailing up the coast of eastern Africa, da Gama ran down a Moslem pilgrim ship carrying worshipers from Mecca. After allowing some children to disembark, he set fire to the ship, and all aboard perished.

After accidentally discovering Japan in 1543 when shipwrecked on one of the islands, the Portuguese quickly established trading stations and Catholic missions, but were eventually expelled in 1638. Above, a Buddhist shrine in Nagasaki; below, a Shinto temple. Left, a group of Portuguese, as depicted by an unknown Japanese artist in the sixteenth century.

Portugal in the twelfth and thirteenth centuries
- Arab-occupied Portuguese territory
- Territory reconquered between 1212 and 1249

PORTUGAL IN THE TWELFTH AND THIRTEENTH CENTURIES

Portugal under the Aviz Dynasty
- Portuguese territory
- Kingdom of Spain (united between 1469 and 1516)

PORTUGAL UNDER THE AVIZ DYNASTY

The Iberian Peninsula from 1580 to 1640
- Kingdom of Spain
- Old Portuguese border

THE IBERIAN PENINSULA FROM 1580 TO 1640

Portugal under the Braganza Dynasty
- Kingdom of Portugal
- Kingdom of Spain

PORTUGAL UNDER THE BRAGANZA DYNASTY

The kingdom of Portugal

The nation of Portugal began as a small realm that broke away from the kingdom of León and Castile in the twelfth century. The early rulers of the nascent country, descendants of a knight from Burgundy, fought Castile, to ensure their independence, and the Moors, to expand the nation southward. By the middle of the thirteenth century, the Burgundian kings had set the borders of modern Portugal.

In the 1380s the House of Aviz came to power under King John I during a war with Castile. Though the Castilians were supported by many Portuguese nobles in their effort to conquer Portugal, John managed to expel the invaders. Portugal's independence would be safe for the next two hundred years.

After the death of the last king of Aviz in 1580, King Philip II of Spain, the son of a Portuguese princess, conquered Portugal—largely through bribing Portuguese nobles. The Spanish ruled Portugal for the next sixty years, until they were ousted in 1640 by a party of nobles under the leadership of John, duke of Braganza, who founded the new royal house.

Portuguese independence was threatened briefly by a Spanish invasion in 1762, and more seriously early in the nineteenth century by the machinations of Napoleon. When Portugal refused to join Napoleon's economic campaign against its long-time ally, England, French forces invaded Portugal in 1807, with the goal of dividing the country between France and Spain. The invasion marked the start of the seven-year Peninsular War, which pitted Portuguese and English forces, commanded by the future duke of Wellington, against the armies of France and Spain. The royal family had fled to Brazil at the outbreak of the war and did not return to Portugal until 1821. In 1832 a two-year civil war, known as the War of the Two Brothers, began a long period of strife between liberal and conservative factions. This struggle continued into the twentieth century, culminating in 1908 with the assassination of King Carlos. His successor, Manuel II, ruled for only two years before fleeing Portugal amidst a revolution.

PORTUGAL OF THE NAVIGATORS
- Portuguese settlement
- Spanish settlement
- Expedition of Bartholomeu Días (1487)
- Expedition of Vasco da Gama (1497)
- Expedition of Pedro Álvares Cabral (1500)
- Line of demarcation according to Treaty of Tordesillas (1494)
- Provisional line of demarcation according to bulls of 1493

Portugal's empire

The seeds of the Portuguese empire were sown as early as the fourteenth century, when King Diniz (reigned 1279–1325), one of medieval Portugal's most remarkable rulers, placed a Genoese sea captain in charge of developing Portugal's navy. With great foresight, he also ordered the Atlantic coastline planted with trees to provide timber for the ocean-going fleets he envisioned in Portugal's future. By 1341 ships flying the Portuguese flag undertook exploration in the Canary Islands, bringing back wood, skins, and tallow. A century later captains under Prince Henry's supervision voyaged down the Atlantic coast of Africa, procuring gold and slaves.

Throughout the fifteenth century, Portuguese ships pressed farther and farther south in search of a sea route to the

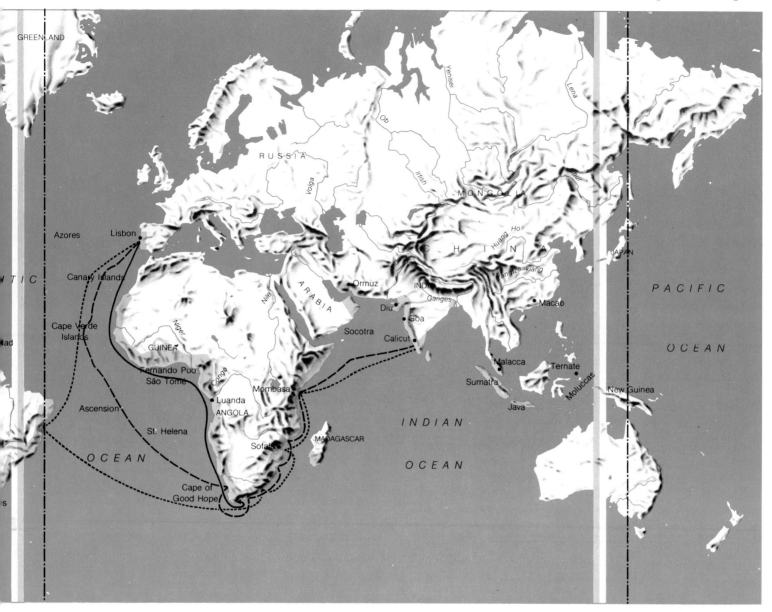

Indies—the source of the spices that Europe sought. Portuguese captains soon became the best in Europe, sailing the most maneuverable ships and applying the latest innovations in the fields of navigation and cartography. After six decades of exploration—during which time Portuguese traders explored all of Africa's Atlantic coast—Bartholomeu Dias rounded the Cape of Good Hope (1488).

Columbus' discovery of America in 1492 created a conflict between the colonial interests of Spain and Portugal. The dispute was resolved in 1494 by the Treaty of Tordesillas, by which a line was drawn around the globe dividing it between the two countries. Four years later Vasco da Gama landed in India, opening a sea lane between Europe and Asia—a milestone in history as significant as Columbus' voyages. Portugal quickly established trading stations along the eastern coast of Africa and in the Indies, China, and Japan.

Pedro Álvares Cabral planted the Portuguese flag in the New World in 1500 when he landed on the shores of Brazil; by the middle of the sixteenth century the coastline was dotted with Portuguese settlements. Successful sugar plantations formed the basis of Brazil's economy until gold was discovered in 1693. Missionaries, slavers, and planters explored Brazil's interior and extended the colony's boundaries beyond the limit set by the Treaty of Tordesillas. In 1750 the territorial gains were recognized by Spain in the Treaty of Madrid, which established the boundaries of modern Brazil.

A world war fought against the Dutch cost Portugal much of its Asian empire in the mid-seventeenth century. In South America, Brazil remained a colony until it declared its independence in September 1822. Portugal's African territories—Portuguese Guinea, Angola, and Mozambique—gained their autonomy in the 1970s.

BRAZIL IN 1784

Viceroyalty of Brazil

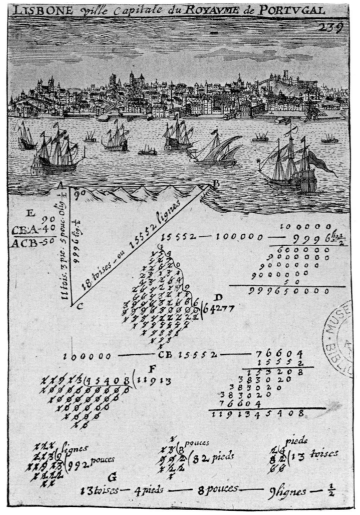

When he arrived at Cochin, da Gama found the city—whose ruler had agreed to trade with the Portuguese—under attack by the Samuri of Calicut. Though the Samuri's forces fled at the appearance of the fleet, da Gama took the precaution of leaving behind a small garrison and a few ships that later beat back several assaults—a success that impressed the princes of the other city-states of southern India, who readily agreed to trade with the Europeans.

Portugal's strategy for establishing its overseas trading empire evolved very quickly and was based not on ideas developed in a vacuum in Lisbon but rather on the political and geographical realities of Africa and Asia. The Portuguese captains observed that the trade in spices and other goods could be taken over if Portugal controlled a few key sea lanes and a string of coastal trading cities. Once they had agreed on a plan, the Portuguese completed it with amazing speed, under the forceful leadership of Viceroy Francisco de Almeida and Governor Afonso de Albuquerque.

The first steps were taken in eastern Africa, where Almeida built forts at the cities of Sofala in 1505 and Mozambique in 1507 and formed an alliance with the ruler of Malindi. When the Egyptians sought to check the rapid Portuguese advance by dispatching a fleet to the Indian coast, they were decisively defeated by Almeida at the battle of Diu in 1509, which virtually assured Portugal a free hand in Indian waters. Almeida's successor, Albuquerque, moved just as swiftly, taking the Indian city of Goa in 1510 and establishing it as Portugal's military and commercial headquarters. The following year Albuquerque gained control of Malacca, a wealthy trading city on the southwestern shore of the Malay Peninsula that overlooked the strait between the peninsula and Sumatra. This channel, through which Portuguese ships fanned out to Java, the Moluccas, Indonesia, and north to Chinese waters, became a popular gateway to the east.

When Portuguese warships tried to force their way into China's coastal cities in 1521 and 1522, they were routed by the imperial navy. But by bribing city officials the persistent Portuguese initiated a semiclandestine trade. In the 1550s a trading station was established at Macao without the knowledge of the emperor, whose officials kept him in the dark about the foreigners' presence for twenty years.

The Portuguese were able to gain a foothold in China partly because of that country's enmity toward the Japanese, whom the Chinese called "the dwarf-

Above far left, an engraving of the harbor on the Tagus River at Lisbon, with measurements of the water's depth. Above, the Tagus today.

This sixteenth-century map (above), by an unknown cartographer, dramatizes the loss of Portugal's independence by juxtaposing the Portuguese flag, flying over Lisbon, with the Spanish royal coat of arms.

King Sebastian I (near left) ascended the Portuguese throne in 1557 at the age of three. Twenty-one years later, in 1578, he led an ill-advised crusade in Morocco, where he was killed in battle, leaving no heir. His great-uncle Henry (this page, far left), a cardinal, succeeded him but died two years later. His death paved the way for Philip II of Spain to claim the Portuguese throne.

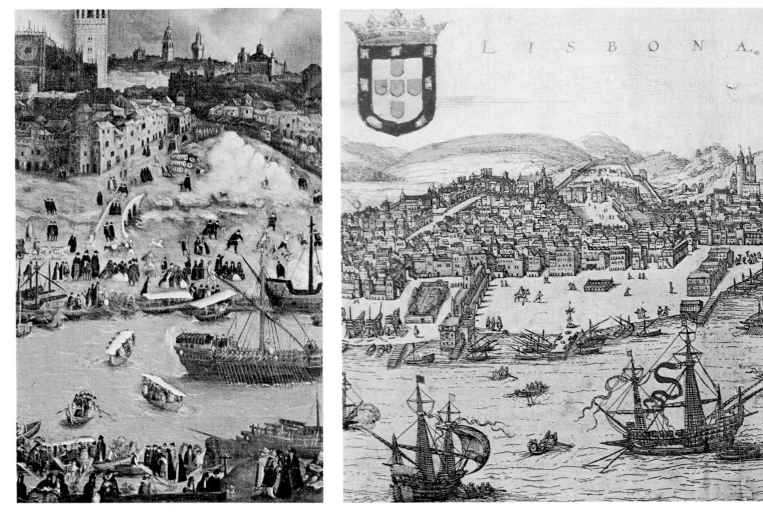

robbers" (a reference to their short stature and unscrupulous trading habits). The Portuguese became the first Europeans to visit Japan, arriving inadvertently in 1543 when a storm drove a trading ship onto the island of Tanegashima. Soon the Portuguese were reaping large profits selling Chinese silk for Japanese silver, since the two great Asian powers could not bear to deal with each other.

The China-Japan trade was just one small thread in a vast web of commerce. The Portuguese gathered pepper from Malabar and Indonesia; mace and nutmeg from the Banda Islands; cloves from the Moluccas; cinnamon from Ceylon; silk and porcelain from China; silver from Japan; horses from Arabia; and sandalwood, verzin, wormwood, mastic, spikenard, borax, camphor, aloes, musk, and civet from far-flung entrepôts. The precious commodities were brought to Goa, which grew into a flourishing marketplace graced with European-style architecture and referred to as Golden Goa. Once a year a fleet of about eight carracks arrived at Goa with silver coins and bullion to pay the empire's suppliers and transport the valuable cargo back to Portugal.

The trade that created Golden Goa did little to improve the lot of most Portuguese citizens at home.

Portugal suffered from the problem of a foreign trade deficit; the spices and Oriental luxuries it sold to other European nations could not quite pay for the silver, copper, grain, arms, and other goods it had to import as a result of undeveloped domestic industry. While the countryside languished, a small group of businessmen and nobles profited from the commerce with Asia, leasing trade rights from the king for particular items in exchange for payment of a flat fee. The fees the monarch received, however, were never enough to compensate for the expenses of outfitting ships and manning the military outposts in Asia. In fact, even as the fruits of empire were filling his capital's warehouses, King Manuel was desperately borrowing money from Portuguese merchants. The Portuguese traders who leased concessions from the Crown sank their profits into land and country houses. Foreign investors removed their revenues to coffers in England, France, Italy, and other countries.

Portugal's economic woes were exacerbated by its persecution of Jewish merchants and moneylenders, whose financial acumen could have helped to create a sound economy. The Christians of Portugal, with the notable exception of King Manuel himself, did not disguise their anti-Semitic leanings, nor did their neighbors in Castile. Early in Manuel's reign thou-

Above, late sixteenth-century engravings of the Spanish port of Seville (left) and Lisbon (right), made when Portugal was ruled by Spain. During the six decades of Spanish rule, much of Portugal's empire in Asia was lost to the onslaughts of the Dutch, who were fighting a war of independence with Spain.

Philip II (right), who ruled Spain from 1556 to 1598, assumed the Portuguese throne in 1580 after Spanish forces swept aside the military opposition. Philip promised the Portuguese a measure of independence, but his guarantees were not honored by his successors, and the Portuguese people grew increasingly restive.

Above left, the façade of a house made of a decorative tile called azulejo. *Azulejos were also used to depict contemporary events. Above, a tile depiction of the 1640 coup led by the duke of Braganza.*

Below, the Gothic castle of the Braganzas at Guimarães. Left, plans of the fortresses of Braga and Portalegre. Their star shape provided strategic advantages and protection against cannon fire.

John IV (above), the duke of Braganza, led the rebellion against the Spanish that put him on the throne in 1640. His reign was characterized by a search for European allies, significant victories over Spain, and continuing struggles with the Dutch. Right, a view of seventeenth-century daily life outside of the Jerónimos Monastery in Belém.

sands of Jews, fleeing persecution in Castile, sought dubious asylum in Portugal. Manuel allowed entry to the refugees after extracting large payments of gold from the unfortunates, but the Castilian princess he was about to marry insisted that he "purify" his nation of the Jews. The Portuguese themselves were alarmed at the sudden influx of Jews, and the increasing religious tension led Manuel to require, in 1497, all Jews to convert to Catholicism or leave the country. Of the twenty thousand Jews in Lisbon, most accepted Christianity, and in return Manuel promised them his protection against discrimination.

But the mass conversion did not mollify the prejudice of the Portuguese, who simply labeled the converts New Christians. In 1506 a Lisbon mob, agitated by a few fanatical priests, killed several hundred New Christians in a three-day riot. Manuel reacted sternly—fifty of the rioters were executed and the ringleaders' monastery was shut—but the king could do little to subdue the deeply rooted hostility of the people.

Religious persecution was institutionalized in 1536 when Manuel's successor, John III—with the reluctant assent of the pope—set up the Holy Office of the Inquisition to investigate the beliefs of the New Christians, testing their renunciation of Judaism.

Untold numbers were dragged before the Inquisitors after they had been denounced as unrepentant Jews. The fortunate ones died in prison. Some 1,500 people were publicly burned at the stake or garroted after confessing under torture to Jewish beliefs. In effect the Inquisition served as an instrument of economic and social repression, as Old Christians in the nobility were able to bring charges against their business rivals in the rising middle class. The Inquisitors confiscated the property of the accused and displaced their families as a matter of routine. Late in the sixteenth century the Inquisition was buttressed by a series of laws curtailing the activities of New Christians and denying them public offices. In the face of this official persecution many wealthy Jewish families left Portugal—having bribed the emigration officials—and settled in London and Amsterdam, where their resources and experience were at the disposal of Portugal's competitors.

The empire's perennial shortage of funds, aggravated by the flow of Jewish wealth out of the country, kept salaries low for soldiers and others serving in Asia and Africa. Often public officials went for months without any pay at all. As a result these officials—who, along with the soldiers, were not of the best character—took to embezzling and smuggling to

Preceding pages, a formation of troops in the square in front of the royal palace in Lisbon. The palace was among many buildings destroyed in the earthquake of 1755. Below, Sebastião José de Carvalho e Mello, better known as the marquis of Pombal. Pombal exercised virtually absolute power from 1755 to 1777. He reformed Portugal's economy and ended oppression of the Jews, but his dictatorship, was marked by ruthless suppression of his opponents and brutal executions. Left, a coin worth twenty thousand reis, minted during the reign of John V.

supplement their meager incomes. Most often they were ne'er-do-wells and criminals, recruited by force in Lisbon and brought to the wharves in chains. More respectable and industrious citizens were reluctant to make the journey to Asia because of its notorious hardships. The voyage, normally lasting six months, exposed the participants to extremes of heat and cold, poor nutrition, and disease that killed as much as half the crew. Shipwrecks took an increasing toll because of the inexperience of the crews, who were sometimes ignorant of the most basic nautical skills. Even the terms "port" and "starboard" confused many crew members, so captains devised a method of hanging onions off one side of the ship and garlic off the other and gave orders referring to the "onion side" and the "garlic side." (Spanish captains had an equally ingenious solution to the problem of giving orders to seamen who literally "didn't know the ropes"; they fastened a playing card to each line and told the tars to "hoist the king of spades" or "pull the two of hearts.")

The same ships that plied Portugal's international trade also carried missionaries, in keeping with the nation's commitment to spreading Christianity. As one Jesuit writer noted, "The preachers take the Gospel and the merchants take the preachers." The first

During the long reign of John V (left), from 1706 to 1750, Portugal's fortunes and international esteem rapidly revived. But the kingdom's wealth derived from gold discoveries in Brazil—not from a sound economy at home. By the end of John's tenure the treasury was empty. There was not even enough money left in the coffers to pay for the king's funeral.

One of the chief reasons for Portugal's financial troubles at the end of John's reign was the king's extravagance. He built a combined palace and monastery (above) in Mafra, at enormous expense, and squandered large sums on royal baubles, such as the carriage below.

missionaries to reach Asia, however, seemed more concerned with gold than with the Gospel. One cleric declared his goal was to amass five thousand cruzados—in addition to as many rubies and pearls as he could obtain—in three years.

The situation changed in 1542 with the arrival in India of the first Jesuit missionaries, among them Saint Francis Xavier, known as the Apostle to the Indies. Better educated and more dedicated than their predecessors, the Jesuits established successful missions throughout the empire. Their attempts at conversion were aided by Portugal's colonial government, which employed legal and, less frequently, mil-

itary tactics to impose Christianity on Asia. These measures included the destruction of mosques and shrines and the banning of Moslem and Hindu religious observances. The missionaries also rounded up Hindu orphans—loosely defined as any children who had lost one of their parents—and placed them in Christian homes. Hindu families were registered by force and required to attend Sunday religious instruction; those who did not were fined. Concerning Asian religious beliefs, almost nothing was sacred to the missionaries. When Portuguese troops seized a holy relic—a tooth supposedly from the body of Buddha himself—the archbishop of Goa publicly hammered it into dust despite the offer of a vast ransom by a Burmese king.

The combination of preaching and punishment won between five hundred thousand and a million converts in Asia. Although the missionaries realized that many of these conversions were based more on fear than faith, they were confident that the children and grandchildren of the converts would grow up as true Christians and, not incidentally, loyal subjects of Portugal.

Portugal's South American colonies in Brazil were developing more slowly than the Asian empire. For the first three decades of the sixteenth century the Portuguese were content to make infrequent visits to the South American coast to trade with the native Indians for novelties like monkeys and parrots and for the more valuable commodity of brazilwood, from which the country derived its name. The Portuguese carried logs of this wood back to Europe where they were reduced to shavings and soaked in water to make a sought-after red dye for clothes. The actions of the French, who were also pursuing this trade (in violation of the Treaty of Tordesillas), encouraged Portugal's King John III to set up permanent settlements in Brazil and oust his competitors from their colony at Rio de Janeiro.

The king divided the coastline into a string of provinces, called captaincies, to be developed by Portuguese gentry. Most of the captaincies failed, but the areas around Rio de Janeiro and the land near Bahia and Pernambuco, on the cental eastern coast, became thriving sugar-producing regions. The Portuguese who found life too harsh in the mother country often settled in these areas in the hope of becoming gentleman planters. These Brazilian pioneers believed that the Indian population would be a ready source of cheap labor. But the Indians were hunters—not farmers—by nature and proved unwilling to work the fields.

The planters resorted to enslaving the Indians, a practice that was outlawed by the Crown and vigorously opposed by Jesuit missionaries, who became

From the beginning of his two decades of dictatorial rule, the marquis of Pombal sought to reduce the power of the nobility and the Jesuits. His machinations culminated in the brutal execution (above right) of seven nobles and three of their servants on charges of attempting to kill King Joseph (reigned 1750–1777). The Jesuits were also implicated in the plot, leading to the execution of one priest, the imprisonment of 124 others, and the expulsion of the religious order from Portugal and the colonies.

Top, persons accused of religious crimes by the Inquisition—an ecclesiastical tribunal set up by Portugal's John III—being paraded through a Lisbon square. The condemned were publicly burned at the stake (left)—a practice later outlawed by the dictator Pombal. Immediately above, a Bible on which witnesses were asked to swear during the Inquisition's hearings.

their protectors. In the face of these obstacles and the passive resistance of the natives, the planters began to import thousands of African slaves, ignoring the king's attempts to discourage African slavery. The slave trade kept pace with the rapid growth of the Brazilian sugar trade between 1575 and 1600, by which time the colonies at Bahia and Pernambuco had reached a height of prosperity rivaling that of Lisbon itself.

The influx of settlers produced an unforeseen and catastrophic effect on the natives, in addition to the obvious hardships of slavery. When the Portuguese first arrived in Brazil, they were astonished at the robust health of the Indians, who never suffered from the countless diseases that afflicted Europe. Soon, however, smallpox, plague, and a virulent form of dysentery claimed the lives of hundreds of thousands of Indians. Although the Jesuit missionaries fought the onslaught of these imported diseases, the medical science of the time was completely useless: The Indians treated the diseases by wrapping the victims in leaves and warming them near fires—a method that appalled the Jesuits, who substituted their own, equally ineffective, therapy of bleeding. The white man's diseases proved to be the hidden curse of European expansionism.

During the time that the Portuguese Empire was reaching a peak of power and wealth, dynastic problems nearly proved its undoing. With the death of John III in 1557, the crown passed to his grandson, Sebastian, who was only three years old and already afflicted with a disease that was to make him impotent. As Sebastian grew older he demonstrated no affection for women, even recoiling at the suggestion of marriage. "Talking to [the king] of marriage is like talking to him of death," observed the Spanish ambassador at the Lisbon court, which was uneasy about the slim prospects of an heir. Sebastian's courtiers grew even more apprehensive when he talked of launching yet another crusade in Morocco, already the graveyard of thousands of Portuguese knights. Encouraged by ambitious flatterers at the court, Sebastian led an army of some twenty-three thousand soldiers into disaster in Morocco at the 1578 Battle of the Three Kings. Although Sebastian was killed there, the amazed Portuguese people refused to believe he was dead. Several impostors appeared, only to be executed or sentenced to slavery. Nonetheless the people's faith in Sebastian's ultimate return remained unshaken and eventually evolved into a mystical cult that persisted into the nineteenth century. Foreign visitors derisively joked that half of Portugal

Above, the Portuguese defenses on the island of Timor in Indonesia, which was in Portuguese hands until 1975.

Left and above, two views of the fort of San Sebastian, which Francisco de Almeida began building in Mozambique in 1507. That city grew into one of the most important Portuguese trading stations in eastern Africa.

Right, a 1610 water color of the Hooghly River at the town of Hooghly. Located twenty-two miles north of Calcutta, Hooghly was established by the Portuguese as an important Indian trading post in 1537.

149

was waiting for the coming of the Messiah and the other half for Sebastian.

Sebastian was succeeded by his great-uncle, an aged cardinal, who lived to rule for only two years. During this time, the Spanish king, Philip II, had been assiduously preparing for the cardinal's death. Philip's agents spread bribes and promises among Portugal's nobles to gain backing for his plan to unite the two Iberian nations under the Spanish Crown; thus little resistance was offered when Philip invaded Portugal in 1580. The following year the Cortes, Portugal's legislative assembly, accepted him as Philip I of Portugal, assenting to the Spanish rule that would last for six decades.

The union proved a disaster for the empire, as Portugal became embroiled in Spain's conflict with the Dutch. Beginning in 1567, Philip, who had been given sovereignty over the Netherlands by his father, Holy Roman Emperor Charles V, was faced with years of revolt by several Dutch provinces, which were receiving the support of England. In 1588, Philip tried to invade England, launching a combined Spanish-Portuguese fleet—the Invincible Armada. The defeat of the Armada by the English dealt a devastating blow to Portugal's navy, which Philip was unable to rebuild.

In the hope of crippling the economy of the insurgent provinces, Philip closed Lisbon to Dutch ships. The embargo, however, had the opposite effect for it compelled the Dutch to circumvent Portugal's monopoly on Asian goods. A Dutchman who had served the Portuguese guided some rebel ships to the Indian Ocean late in the sixteenth century. There they found that Portugal's grip on its empire was faltering. Its military and trading outposts were vulnerable to attack by sea; its colonies were exposed by the defeat of the navy and unprotected by an occupying army or loyal populace. The few troops available were notoriously undisciplined, and their officers largely incompetent.

Above right, the Mogul emperor Jahangir, who ruled from 1605 to 1627. The Mogul Empire stretched from central India to Afghanistan but did not threaten the coastal cities where the Portuguese had their trading centers. The Moguls were in fact friendly toward Europeans; Jahangir extended trading privileges to both the Portuguese and the British, and his father, Akbar, asked the Portuguese to send missionaries to his Moslem realm. In 1683 the Moguls attacked an army of Hindu Marathas that was about to besiege Portuguese Goa (right), saving the city from certain destruction.

Goa, on the western coast of India, served as the headquarters for Portugal's entire Asian empire. The cathedral of Panjim (above) in Goa has a distinctly European architectural style. Top right, a relief covered with gold laminate, in another Goa church. Above right, a landscape just outside the city.

Portugal's military disarray was irreversible, and the Dutch exploited it to the utmost. They attacked the length and breadth of the empire, beginning with raids in Africa in 1598. The ensuing war, which lasted until 1663, was fought on three continents—Africa, Asia, and South America—from Indonesia to Peru. The vast geographic scope of the war and the number of peoples embroiled in its battles—the English, Danes, Persians, Indonesians, Cambodians, Japanese, Africans, and American Indians—have led the noted historian Charles Boxer to call this conflict the first world war.

Despite its seemingly fatal weaknesses, the Portu-

India

India was not a "new world" to the Portuguese when Vasco da Gama landed there in 1498. It had been mentioned by classical writers as well as in the accounts of Arab and European travelers. Even so, the Portuguese had little reliable information about that distant country. Judging from the paltry gifts the explorers brought for India's rulers, the Portuguese may have thought they would find a primitive people. The Portuguese also assumed that the Indians were Christians and, at first, mistook the Hindu temples for churches. Once the newcomers discovered their error, they proceeded to demolish many Indian temples and convert the Indians, often against their will. The governors also forbade all non-Christian rites and rituals and encouraged their men to marry Indian women, despite the Hindus' aversion to mixed marriages. The policies of mass conversion to Christianity and intermarriage created a populace in the coastal trading cities that remained under Portuguese influence for centuries.

Indian women (right) bathe in a pool with their children. The women were probably members of a harem in the household of a Moslem potentate, or ruler. Top, a blacksmith shop on the outskirts of an Indian village. The illustrations on these pages, with the exception of the one in the lower right-hand corner, are from an early-sixteenth-century Portuguese book about the everyday life of the Indians. The scene at far right is from an Italian work.

Above, center and right, scenes of farming and herding in India. Though the Hindus considered oxen sacred animals, their beliefs did not prevent them from using the animals as beasts of burden.

Two Indian women (below) sit by a tree as a boy climbs for fruit.

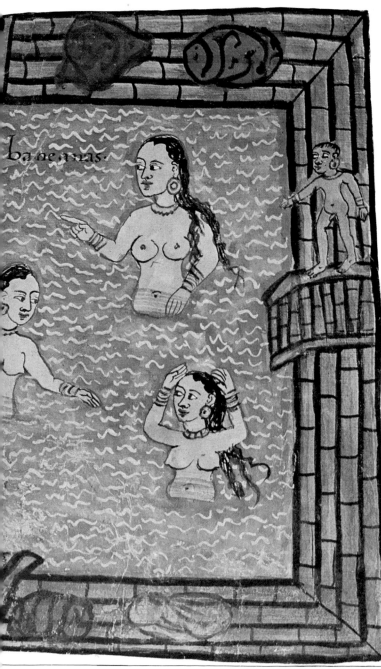

Far right, Count Francisco Xavier de Tavora, governor of Rio de Janeiro from 1712 to 1716. Right, Luis de Vasconcelos e Sousa, viceroy of Brazil from 1779 to 1790. He was responsible for suppressing a republican conspiracy in 1789 under a popular leader called Tiradentes (the Toothpuller).

Left, a painting of one of the two battles of Guararapes. In these battles of 1648 and 1649, Portuguese armies, consisting largely of Indians and Africans, decisively defeated Dutch forces.

guese Empire tottered but did not fall. By the 1620s the Portuguese realized that much of their Asian empire was indefensible, as well as expensive to maintain, draining the nation's strength. Thus they abandoned these colonies in order to concentrate their forces in Brazil. By the 1660s Portugal's Asian possessions were reduced to Goa, Diu, and a few other spots on the Indian coast; Macao, on the southeastern coast of China; and part of the island of Timor in Indonesia. In Africa, the Portuguese repelled the Dutch from Mozambique and defeated them in Angola with a relief force from Brazil. The Dutch were also driven out of northeastern Brazil in bitter fighting, including the battles at Guararapes in 1648 and 1649.

While Portugal was losing ground in some areas to the onslaughts of the Dutch overseas, patriotic forces at home were gaining strength. In the late 1630s a party of Portuguese nobles laid plans to oust the Spanish, selecting John, the duke of Braganza, as their leader and candidate for the throne. While Philip IV was preoccupied by a war with France and rebellions in Sicily and the Spanish province of Catalonia in 1640, the Portuguese patriots overwhelmed the Spanish garrisons in Lisbon and proclaimed King John IV their leader.

Portugal underwent a rapid revival after it made peace with the Dutch in 1663. The Dutch war had been a costly one; but the greatest loss, involving many of the Asian colonies, may have been a disguised blessing for the empire as a whole. By the 1660s Portugal was free to focus on Brazil, which was thriving. As early as the 1630s, groups of explorers called *bandeiras* were venturing into the interior of the South American continent, where they successfully contended with the Spanish for territories beyond the limits of the 1494 Treaty of Tordesillas. Together with the efforts of missionaries in the north, the explorations of the bandeiras more or less established Portuguese boundaries of modern Brazil by the late 1630s, although these boundaries were not officially recognized by Spain until 1750.

Perhaps the greatest achievement of the bandeiras was their discovery of gold in the 1690s, about two hundred miles west of São Paulo—a discovery that touched off the first modern gold rush. The region where the gold was found was called Minas Gerais, or the General Mines. It quickly became the bedrock, or, perhaps more accurately, the cane of Portugal's chronically shaky economy.

Though the flow of gold from Brazil once again made Lisbon an important trading center during the reign of Pedro II (1683-1706), social and religious problems continued to hinder economic development. These problems were set forth by a committee of Lisbon merchants in an illuminating letter to the king:

> Without trade, there is not a kingdom which is not poor, not a republic which is not famished. Yet in this capital city of your Majesty, the merchants are so little favored, and commerce is despised to such a degree, that men are discouraged from becoming traders ... since they see with their own eyes that to the Portuguese a merchant is no better than a fish-porter. This is the reason why there are so few Portuguese merchants in

Traffic in slaves

In large part, the Portuguese Empire was built and maintained by slave labor. The sale of slaves on the European market made Portugal's fifteenth-century voyages profitable. In the sixteenth century, when Portuguese manpower was short, the empire relied on crews of African and Asian slaves to sail its ships between India and the homeland. The importation of slaves was crucial to the development of the Brazilian colony because of prohibitions by both the Portuguese government and the Catholic Church against the enslavement of South American Indians and the unwillingness of the Indians to work the mines and plantations.

By the 1570s these developments, combined with the burgeoning sugar industry in Brazil, led to an intensification of slave traffic between that colony and Africa. The discovery of gold in Brazil in the 1690s further increased the demand for slaves, resulting in the importation of roughly 1,800,000 slaves between 1700 and 1810. This enormous immigration to the Minas Gerais (General Mines) district created a population in the early nineteenth century in which as many as one half of the people were slaves. The slave traffic was abolished by Brazil in 1831 but the slaves already residing there were not freed until 1888, when all seven hundred thousand were emancipated.

Top center, a 1775 map of Brazil's Minas Gerais district. The engravings on these pages show scenes of slave life in Brazil in the early part of the nineteenth century. Top left, a capitão da mata—*captain of the woods—whose job was to search out runaway slaves. Top, far right, slaves in the hold of a ship on the Atlantic crossing. Center, far right, slaves landing at Rio de Janeiro, where the slave markets (bottom, far right) were located. All three engravings are by Jean-Baptiste Debret. Near right, slaves working on a coffee plantation, from Rugendas'* Gathering Coffee Beans, Near Rio.

this kingdom, and why so many foreigners of all nations swarm here, who are the bloodsuckers of all your Majesty's money.

The authors of this letter tactfully avoided any mention of the basis of Portuguese antipathy toward merchants—namely the belief that all merchants were New Christians. Since young Portuguese men were reluctant to enter such a despised career, the vacuum was filled by foreign traders, mostly English, who indeed swarmed over Lisbon. Many of these foreigners were agents for companies set up by Portuguese Jews who had emigrated to more tolerant capitals. The ever-vigilant Inquisition continued to harass New Christians, the only group with the financial reserves necessary for funding large projects. In the 1640s King John IV had been forced to promise that investments in the Crown's new trading company, Brazil House, would be immune from confiscation by the Inquisition to attract the backing of New Christians.

Since domestic funds to spur the economy were lacking, Portugal fastened its hopes on the Brazilian gold mines. But much of the Brazilian gold destined for Portugal's treasury made only a courtesy call at Lisbon. The Portuguese gold traders, forbidden by law from exporting the metal, clandestinely handed it over to English traders at Lisbon in exchange for merchandise. England's profit on this surreptitious trade was so great, and Portugal's loss so large, that a Portuguese diplomat wrote in despair that his country had become "the best and most profitable colony of England."

Pedro's successor, John V, turned a blind eye to the nation's economic troubles, spending money as fast as it arrived from Brazil merely to erect a dazzling façade of regal wealth and power. John bestowed lavish gifts on the Church, established three libraries, regularly gave gold coins away to the poor, and con-

During his reign, from 1750 to 1777, King Joseph I (above) handed control of the country over to his chief minister, the marquis of Pombal. Pombal's opponents attempted to assassinate Joseph in 1758. Gunmen in ambush fired on the king's carriage but Joseph managed to escape. Although the attackers were not caught, Pombal ordered the arrest of several nobles, many of whom were executed after secret trials.

The Lisbon earthquake

On November 1, 1755, three violent tremors wrecked two thirds of Lisbon (see picture at right) and killed between ten and fifteen thousand people. More destruction followed when a tidal wave roared down the Tagus River, swamping the dock areas where many survivors had taken refuge. The shock of the earthquake was felt as far away as Gdańsk, Poland; the tidal wave reached islands in the Caribbean that same day.

The disaster also had scientific repercussions. All over Europe scientists and priests debated the cause of the quake. In the face of a widespread belief that the calamity expressed divine wrath, scientists promoted the more rational idea that the tremors were caused by natural forces, which could be explained by systematic investigation.

Above, one of the twelve Prophets on the stairway of a church in Minas Gerais, Brazil. The statues are the work of Antonio Francisco Lisboa, known as Aleijadinho—Little Cripple— because a disease cost him the use of his hands and feet. He worked with a hammer and chisel strapped to his arms.

Right, the church of St. Francis of Assisi in Minas Gerais, built in 1762. The district of Minas Gerais enjoyed great prosperity in the eighteenth century because of its rich gold mines.

The wealthy Brazilian trading city of Bahia was protected by the formidable bastion of São Marcelo (left), built in 1623. Bahia was Brazil's colonial capital from 1549 to 1762.

159

Coimbra

The first capital of Portugal was not Lisbon, but the ancient city of Coimbra, which was an important town as early as the first century B.C. The city is best known for Portugal's oldest university, founded in Lisbon in 1292 by King Diniz, and moved permanently to its present home in 1537. Its sixteenth-century curriculum included law, rhetoric, mathematics, theology, medicine, grammar, and Greek. In 1550 the student body numbered about fifteen hundred, and the faculty included eminent professors from Paris. When the university ran afoul of the Inquisition in 1558, its administration was partly taken over by the Jesuits to guarantee orthodoxy.

In the eighteenth century the marquis of Pombal took a personal interest in reforming Coimbra's curriculum. He undertook a building program, established a faculty of natural science, and opened laboratories, a museum, a botanical garden, and an observatory. Pombal's campaign against the Jesuits included the closing of their university at Évora, which made Coimbra the sole institution of higher learning in the country until 1911.

Above, a map of Coimbra drawn in the early nineteenth century. The university is set on the heights above the city, along with a twelfth-century cathedral. The city, located on the Mondego River, was the capital of Portugal and residence of its kings from 1139 to 1260.

The library of the university (left) was built between 1718 and 1728 by John V, who financed the project with Brazilian gold. Below, the main entrance to the university.

John VI (right) ascended the throne in 1816 while in exile in Brazil. Because his mother, Queen Maria I, was insane, he had already served as regent for sixteen years. On his return to Lisbon in 1821, John was forced to accept the liberal constitution that had been drawn up in his absence.

Left, two portraits of Joanquina Carlota de Borbón, the fiery queen of John VI. The lower portrait was painted by Jean-Baptiste Debret during the royal family's stay in Brazil.

structed a palace at Mafra, outside of Lisbon, a gigantic project that strained the economy and took nearly twenty years to complete. An even greater monument was the Aqueduct of Free Waters, which brought a sufficient supply of drinking water to the capital for the first time. John had to pay for the aqueduct with a new tax, because his Mafra palace had depleted the treasury. When John died in 1750 his officials were forced to scrape and borrow to pay for the funeral.

Portugal's economic tribulations were still in evidence when John's successor, Joseph I, ascended the throne in 1750. The decline in fortunes was soon reversed, however, not by the king, but by his infamous,

Above left, the wharves in the industrial quarter of eastern Lisbon, known as Xabregas. The print was made around 1800, during the regency of Prince John. Left, a view of the Jewish section of the capital, where the residents placed statues of the Virgin on their balconies to deflect the enmity of Lisbon's Christian citizens. The marquis of Pombal had repealed all anti-Semitic laws during his dictatorship—a move that had curious repercussions abroad, as other Europeans concluded that all Portuguese were secret Jews.

all-powerful minister, the marquis of Pombal. One modern commentator has called Pombal "an extraordinary Jekyll-and-Hyde character"—an apt description of a man whose career combined admirable, humanitarian achievements and economic acumen with acts of terror and repression.

Pombal began his career as a minor player in Portuguese affairs, as a striver, eager for high office, but distrusted by King John V, who referred to Pombal as having "a hairy heart"—an expressive if ambiguous phrase. Appointed secretary of state for war and foreign affairs by Joseph I, Pombal came to prominence for his deft handling of the crisis following the famous Lisbon earthquake of 1755. While the king was paralyzed by panic in the days following the disaster, Pombal bluntly advised him to "bury the dead and feed the living," and persuaded the king not to abandon his capital. Pombal then issued a stream of orders that brought an end to the chaos. When the crisis had passed he emerged pre-eminent among the country's officers. Not one to underplay his accomplishments, Pombal had a deluxe edition of his earthquake orders printed up and distributed to a select audience.

Pombal's handling of Portugal's economic crisis of the 1760s was equally skillful but was steeped in

Early nineteenth-century Brazil

Brazil had been the jewel of Portugal's empire for over a century when the royal family, fleeing Napoleon's armies, arrived in 1808. The unexpected presence of the king bolstered the colony's fortunes even further. The populace suddenly acquired a sense of independence which was just as quickly spurred by economic developments. Whereas Portugal had formerly enjoyed a monopoly, Brazil's ports were thrown open to trade with all of Europe. New industries sprang up; European scholars, artists, and skilled workers were encouraged to immigrate.

As the economy surged, the national spirit of self-reliance grew with it, and could not be curbed when John VI reluctantly returned to Portugal in 1821. His son Pedro, later crowned Pedro I of Brazil, moved swiftly to consolidate his control of the colony and established its independence in 1822.

Shortly after having declared Brazil's independence on September 7, 1822, John VI's son Pedro (below) is acclaimed by a crowd at the royal palace in Rio de Janeiro. Two years later the United States became the first country to recognize the new nation. Below right, a depiction of Indian life in Brazil engraved by Jean-Baptiste Debret, who also made the engravings on the facing page.

Above, a nineteenth-century engraving of the imperial palace of Brazil's emperor Pedro II in Petrópolis. This settlement, twenty-seven miles north of Rio de Janeiro, was founded in 1845 by German immigrants and underwent rapid growth. Designed by the French architect Vauthier, the summer palace is now a museum of imperial art and artifacts.

Above, a traveling coffee salesman in a small village. Right, an official reading a government proclamation.

Cattle-raising (center right) was an important part of Brazil's economy in the nineteenth century. Bottom right, oxen pulling carts.

Pedro is cheered by a crowd in Brazil (above) soon after having declared the colony's independence. Left, the arrival in Rio de Janeiro of Maria Leopoldina (above left), Pedro's bride.

Far right, Pedro I, emperor of Brazil. Pedro was crowned in December of 1822, roughly a year and a half after his father, John VI of Portugal, had left Brazil for the homeland, ending the royal family's fourteen years of exile. Pedro's first year of rule was despotic but he was persuaded in 1824 to accept a liberal constitution (near right) that limited his powers.

ruthlessness. In the face of a burgeoning foreign trade deficit that was plunging Portugal into a depression, Pombal revived the country's industries and agriculture and set up official trading companies with tight monopolies, to the disadvantage of English and Portuguese private traders. When vineyard workers demonstrated against Pombal's acts he summarily ordered them to their death. When the august Lisbon Chamber of Commerce also opposed his moves, its members were either imprisoned or exiled.

With none daring to oppose him, Pombal upset centuries of tradition by championing the Jews, sweeping away all the old anti-Semitic laws, and muzzling the Inquisition. At the same time he instigated a fanatical persecution of the Jesuits, claiming they were the architects of a worldwide conspiracy against Portugal. Pombal was furious at the Jesuits in Brazil, for example, for protecting the South American Indians from the Portuguese plantation owners, an act which he construed as an attempt to undermine Portuguese efforts at colonization. The Jesuits subsequently were expelled from Portugal and its colonies. Pombal's religious and economic policies naturally aroused powerful enemies, and after the death of his protector, King Joseph, he was removed from his post and banished by Queen Maria I.

Toward the end of Maria's reign (1777–1816), Portugal was threatened by the designs of France's Napoleon, who conspired with the Spanish to carve up the country between them. A French army under Spanish command invaded Portugal in 1807, forcing the royal family to flee on British ships to Brazil, where they remained for fourteen years. The British staved off three invasions of Portugal before peace was finally established with the French in 1814.

The long absence of the royal family allowed a powerful liberal party to take root in Portugal. When John VI returned from Brazil in 1821, he was compelled to consent to a constitutional monarchy: Royal powers were limited by a constitution that declared all citizens equal, ended the privileges of the nobility, and, most important, bestowed the greatest power on the legislature. The political situation was far from resolved, however, and for the rest of the century Portugal was torn by civil wars and internal strife.

John had left his son Pedro behind in Brazil, where Pedro declared himself emperor and Brazil an independent state in 1822. With the loss of Brazil, the African colonies became the most important in the empire. Unlike Brazil, Angola and Mozambique were still largely coastal settlements in the first half of the nineteenth century.

The famous travels through Africa by the Scottish missionary David Livingstone focused Europe's attention on the Dark Continent in the second half of the century. Britain, Belgium, and Germany suddenly laid plans to plant colonies there. Fearful of losing out in the "scramble for Africa," as historians have called this sudden flurry of colonialist activity, Portugal dispatched explorers to the little-known regions between Mozambique and Angola with orders to establish forts there and win the tribesmen over to Portugal's cause. In 1887 the government published the celebrated Rose-colored Map, depicting a single large Portuguese colony stretching from the Atlantic to the Indian Ocean in southern Africa, a claim that collided with British interest in the area. In 1890 the British presented the newly crowned Portuguese king Carlos with an ultimatum—abandon the "rose-colored" scheme or face a break in relations. Fearful that defiance might lead to war, Carlos capitulated. The two nations negotiated their claims in Africa and agreed on the boundaries that Angola and Mozambique have today.

Portugal's empire outlived its monarchy by over sixty years. In 1910 republican forces overthrew King Manuel II, the last monarch of the House of Braganza. The nation's stubborn economic problems led to the rise of Antonio de Oliveira Salazar, who ruled with dictatorial powers from 1932 to 1968. Salazar's regime actually did little to improve Portugal's plight, as he resisted modernizing industry and agriculture for fear of unleashing class conflicts. Thus the nation languished, but held on to its empire despite the growing strength of nationalist movements in Africa. Not only were the colonies important markets for Portugal's exports, but they were also a prop for the national psyche and the prestige of the regime.

The final chapter of Portugal's imperial history began in 1961, when India seized the territories of Goa, Daman, and Diu. Later, as African guerrilla armies in Angola and Mozambique launched bloody campaigns of liberation, Portuguese progressives realized that the colonial period had to be hastened to its end. One of the policies of the military junta that ousted Portugal's conservative regime in 1974 was that of decolonization. By the following year the African colonies were independent. That same year Portugal also relinquished its half of the island of Timor, retaining only Macao, Madeira, and the Azores as the last survivors of imperial glory.

Photography Credits

Index